OF POTS & PANS & POETRY

(AND PUPPIES, PONIES & PUSSY CATS)

LEE F. DOUGLAS

PublishAmerica
Baltimore

ISBN: 1-60836-895-5
PUBLISHED BY PUBLISHAMERICA, LLLP
www.publishamerica.com
Baltimore

Printed in the United States of America

The Best of All Things
To You & yours
Lee Douglas
Jan 29:11

Mick + Lor —
good eating to ya
always —
love ya both —
Ron

DEDICATION

After our mother died when I was three years old, my brothers and I were taken in by our paternal grandparents living in the small town of Alba, Texas.

They were in their early 60's and the only source of income was what was then known as "old age pension checks." Thus it was imperative that the garden behind the house was successful each summer. If it rained too much or too little, or it was too hot or too cold, then there would be enough to can for the winter months.

After my older brother went into the Navy during WWII, my grandfather died and my other brother went into the Navy, it was just "Grandma" and me to tend the garden and preserve the vegetables.

There were many times when the only thing we would have for 'supper' was a glass of buttermilk and leftover cornbread. However, there was always something to take the hunger away.

When I graduated from high school and went into the Navy myself, I was 5' 2" tall and weighed 120 pounds.

During the eleven weeks I was in boot camp, I grew 4" in height and gained 40 pounds in weight. I did not know people ate three meals a day. I never saw so much food.

So began my interest in food which has grown into an obsession of creating new tastes, combining ingredients and seasonings in new ways.

During my most remembered formative years, my grandmother was my guide and only source of comfort and encouragement.

It was also from my grandmother that I learned the art of story telling. Evenings, before we even had a radio, we would sit around and she would tell us stories about when she was growing up and the flavors of her time came through in wonderful word pictures. A favorite time would be when a Texas spring storm would blow through. With enough warning, many of the close neighbors would gather at her house because there was a large storm cellar in the front yard. If the storm got bad enough we would all go in it. Grandpa would sit at the door and hold the rope to keep the door from being blown open. Sitting in the light of kerosene lamps in the house or kerosene lanterns in the storm cellar, always provided the perfect ambiance for the telling of ghost stories; and it took only a little prodding from one of the children to get them started. My children grew up listening to the stories I remembered from those times. Moreover, they remember many of them today. They came in handy when I would took a group of boys camping during the times I was pastoring.

Memories of her still affect my thoughts and actions to this very day and it is to:

Martha Lavonia Davis Douglas

I dedicate, not only this book…
but every achievement in my life.
Lee Douglas

ACKNOWLEDGMENTS

It is always so risky when compiling the list of those who have helped in any project. There are so many subtle ways in which one is indebted to so many people in so many ways; it is practically impossible to remember everyone when faced with the task of making a list.

Favorite foods cooked by favorite people in my life have been a major influence. Lola Mae (England) Harris, a neighbor of my grandmother's, was a great cook who acquired her skills under the tutelage of her mother, Opal England, and fed me many times when I was hungry. She was an early contributor to my appreciation of properly prepared dishes.

Mama Mac, (Merle McReynolds,) a lady I adopted as a grandmother for my children when I was pastor of the Gribble Springs Baptist Church north of Denton, Texas, taught me much as (over her many protestations) I insisted on helping her in the kitchen. She was amazing. Many times she and Bill would invite my family for lunch after church; and the first time I was taken aback when there was nothing ready when we arrived. Forty-five minutes later there were two meats, five vegetables and three desserts on the table. I never figured out how she did it but learned that the secret to good food was to not be sparing with the seasonings.

Up front of those who are responsible for the actual completion of this book are Dallas residents: Tom & M.L. Clifford, Jeff Green, Reg & Elaine Gregory, James & Pat Mitchell; Dr. Arryl Paul of El Paso; Terry & Dina Schoof of Grand Junction, Colorado; Steve Shoultz, Les & Lynn Walters and Emory & Pat White, also of Dallas. They comprise a group of friends and associates who believed in the idea.

Too many to list here (and to remember) are relatives, friends and neighbors who were brave to the extent they agreed to taste test each new recipe.

In the compilation of the stories, recipes and poetry, an incredible debt is due to Jean Hawkins, whose infinite patience with me knew few bounds as I dedicated time and attention to the writing. Her input into the recipes; the reading and correcting of my horrible grammar in the stories and poetry; her encouragement and understanding, has been unending and greatly appreciated.

Then there are dear friends, Terry and Dina Schoof. I remember where we first met, but do not remember not having them for friends. Dina used her incredible talent and applied dedicated effort in reading, correcting, and then re-editing during the early days when there were so many errors. I also owe much to Terry, for his patience and understanding with her as she took family time to read and edit. Through those days before we even knew if it would be accepted by a publisher, they continued to encourage me when my mind got tired. To each is given my continuing appreciation for their friendship.

Pat & Emory White came to the rescue in the final days before publication. Pat is a talented and accomplished gourmet cook, and she and Emory entertain their many friends from around the world with her dinners. They have been a rich source of encouragement by enthusiastically testing recipes and recommending changes as well as contributing ideas for new ones. As we entered the days of final manuscript editing, they each took a weekend out of their busy schedule to attend to the final reading and made multiple suggestions. I owe them an un-payable debt of gratitude.

To everyone at Publish America, thanks for taking a chance and providing this opportunity.

How the Cooking Got Started

"Since I began cooking, it has been my intention to create food that leaves a warm, full feeling in the stomach...and in the heart."
Lee (the Dr.) Douglas

- - - - - - - - -

Some of these recipes have come to me from my grandmother, to whom I have dedicated this collection. Others have come about as acts of desperation.

My recipe for chili, for example, came about as the result of my having made a statement purely as a joke.

I was teaching a Sunday Bible class of older adults at the Northway Christian Church in Dallas, Texas where they had an annual event featuring chili made by one of the long time members. He had been providing the chili for years, and *knowing this*, I made the comment that, "I probably make the best chili in the world, but since it is already set, I'll bring the cornbread."

It was on Monday before the chili supper on Saturday that I got a call from the party organizer. "You said you made good chili, didn't you?"

Unsuspectingly, I answered that I did, but Bob already set to bring it and I was going to bring the cornbread.

"Well there has been a change of plans. Bob underwent triple by-pass surgery last night so it looks like you're elected to do the chili."

Well, there I was being confronted with my previous lie. I had never made chili in my life, and only made the statement based on the assurance that *Bob always made it!*

I was standing in line at the grocery store when the call came in on my cell phone, and what to my happy eyes should appear, but *Texas Monthly's, "Chili" Issue.* Without even a bruise to my integrity, I purchased it.

After reading through all the recipes, I was not pleased with the combinations of ingredients of any of them. I next called a couple of friends who I knew made chili to get their recipe.

After reading until my eyes were numb, I decided to create one from scratch by combining what appealed to me from several different recipes.

It was a resounding success, even with two people who never ate chili, after tasting it, ate more than their share. The recipe is included.

In 1980 when I first took it in hand to create and market the Texas Biscuit Baker, I was told by the people who were going to market it that I would need to come up with some recipes to go along with it.

It was at that time I learned that you cannot copyright a recipe. You can copyright a 'book of recipes,' but not an individual recipe.

Therefore, I bought a lot of old recipe books at flea markets, in antique stores and at garage sales and searched through each for recipes that sounded good. When I came across one I liked, I tweaked it for the flavor that appealed to me.

Now, lest you think this is unethical, let me remind you that *"there is no such thing as an original recipe."*

The following story explains.

Many long ago's two cavemen were sitting around their fire at

10

night when a wild hog, trying to escape a bear, ran into their camp. Hitting a tree and knocking itself out, it fell into their fire.

After watching for a time, one of them reached over and tried to pull the hog out of the fire, whereupon some of the meat came off in his hand. After sniffing a little, he tasted it.

Thus the discovery that, "cooked pig is better than raw pig." Since then any recipe that includes pork is but a variation on that original recipe.

Some of the recipes came from my quest to recreate a taste I had experienced in a restaurant. An example of this is the recipe for Chorizo. After eating some Queso Flameado in a Mexican restaurant, I wanted to do that for my friends at home.

I finally found some at a health food store in Dallas, and used it to create a *"Chorizo and Eggs"* recipe for a brunch. It was good and well received so I later visited the store again and picked up a package. Thinking I could possibly make it myself, I read the label.

I quickly put it back when I read that the leading ingredient was, *"pork parts, including salivary glands and lymph nodes."*

Once again I looked through many books. Finding several recipes, I took the parts I liked best and worked with the amounts of each ingredient until I got it just right. The recipe is included.

All in all I have had a wonderful and delicious time experimenting and cooking for friends and relatives. They seemed to have enjoyed it as well. Any time I have called and begun the conversation with, "Ya'll want to come over for…" they've always interrupted with, "Yes! What time should we be there?"

THE BEGINNING OF THE POETRY

I never intended to write poetry. I liked some of what I read, but writing it was not on my agenda.

In 1994 my son Byron and I went to a lecture at Southern Methodist University in Dallas by the British Physicist, Stephen Hawking.

I was so absorbed in what he had to say (though I understood little) the hour and five minutes seemed like ten minutes. I do remember his closing words, however. He said, "*I am continuing to look for a unified theory of the universe.*"

Later that week I made a trip to Philadelphia to do a ***"Dr. Douglas' Wonder Baker®"*** show on the QVC Shopping Network. After the show I caught an earlier flight than planned which took me through Atlanta. Though there was an hour layover to catch a flight back to Dallas, I was still going to get in earlier than scheduled.

When the plane left the Airport in Philadelphia I pulled the tray-table down. Since I was in the middle of moving my residence, I started a list of things I needed to do. After writing three items on my yellow pad, I remembered Stephen's statement concerning a unified theory of the universe and decided to write it out for him.

From the time I began, including a layover in Atlanta and the time it took to arrive in Dallas, I had written the first eleven verses of what I came to refer to as, "*My Epic.*"

Through the years I have added 161 additional verses, and consider I am about two-thirds complete.

"***ONE,***" which follows, contains those first eleven verses. The finished version will provide answers to many questions that have been around for ages.

Be aware of this however. To fully appreciate everything that is included, you must have more than a passing knowledge of the *"Record."*

ONE

Many "long ago's,"
Before all time began,
Before galaxies and stars,
Before worlds and man,

A presence resolved,
To provide a beginning.
In our struggle to comprehend,
There may be no winning.

Did the presence speak?
Or did it merely think?
Did it take a billion years?
Or happen in a blink?

Could it be a bit of both?
Or possibly neither?
In our quest for understanding,
Must it be either?

The presence looked about,
And saw a likely spot,
As a habitat for angels,
And picked a certain lot.

"This is yours," the presence said,
"Have it as your own,
Do with it as you will
But it's only yours on loan."

"I must be off but will return,
To see how you have fared,
I'll want a full report, of course,
I'll want to know you cared."

"It seems a proper place,
To let you prove your worth"
"What is its name?" I hear you ask,
"Suppose we call it earth."

The presence went away,
There was much yet to be done,
What was needed was some help,
Perhaps, some day a son?

The universe was growing,
So quick, so bright and vast.
Whether by thought, or word, or action,
The die had now been cast.

The being left in charge of earth,
Nothing did he lack.
He tread on diamonds on his way out,
And rubies on his way back.

Many servants he did have,
Attending his every need.
He was lord and master over all,
But it only fed his greed.

Stretched out before him,
As far as eye could see,
Was every flower, grass and bush,
As well as every tree.

Under his foot was every jewel,
Much silver and much gold,
Yet in his pride, he was not satisfied,
In the record it is told.

"I'm only prince of this measly world,
When I should be over all.
I'll rise above this pitiful place,"
And to battle his servants did call.

"It may take a little while,
But I'll conquer all in time,"
So out he went, all hell bent,
And committed his first crime.

Across the whole of the universe,
Rang the sound of a mighty war.
But he who would have conquered all,
Was much the weaker by far.

Back to the earth he was pushed,
He and all his kind.
And to the earth the presence came,
And the servants' powers did bind.

"Here you are, and here you'll stay,"
The presence did demand.
"It's still your world, but here you'll stay,
This is my first command."

"I'm disappointed, you devil you,
I cannot now say more,
I must be off, but I will return,
And your punishment will be sore."

The devil's cries rang across the void,
As to the earth he fell.
"Lord of only this?" he exclaimed,
"I'd rather be lord of hell."

Cast down to earth for evermore,
The devil was not happy
It can be said, you'll understand,
His attitude was crappy.

APPETIZERS & DIPS

Aleppo Spread

1   Cup mayonnaise (or salad dressing)
1   Tsp Aleppo pepper
2   Tsp lemon juice
½   Tsp granulated garlic
½   Tsp **Baja Adobo** seasoning

Mix all together and let set overnight. This is excellent on sandwiches of all kinds and dip for various appetizers.

BLT Spread

1   Lb. bacon, cooked, crumbled
1   Cup light mayonnaise
1   Cup light sour cream
1   Tsp **Baja Adobo** seasoning
1   Tsp **Deep South Soul** seasoning

Combine all ingredients. Chill until ready to serve. Serve with assorted crackers or vegetables.

CHEESE BALLS

4   Cups Bisquick
2   Lb hot breakfast sausage
1   Lb sharp cheddar cheese, grated

Mix all together and roll into 1" balls. If too dry, add a little water. Bake at 250° or until brown.

CHEESE WRAPS

½   Lb Co-jack cheese, grated
½   Lb Cheddar cheese, grated
½   Lb Mozzarella cheese, grated
½   Cup mayonnaise
1   4-oz can chopped green chilies
1   4-oz can chopped pimentos
1   Anaheim pepper, chopped
1   Poblano pepper, chopped
½   Cup sweet onion, chopped
1   Tbs **Baja Adobo** seasoning

Put all ingredients into oven-proof dish, mix well and bake at 425° until cheese is well melted together.

Take out of oven and spread on flour tortillas, roll and slice. Serve while hot.

CHICKEN AND BACON WRAPS

1   Cup vegetable cream cheese
1   10-oz can chunk chicken breast
½   Cup crumbled crisp-fried bacon
½   Tsp **New Mexico Chipotle** seasoning.
½   Cup medium Picante Salsa
6   8-inch soft flour tortillas

Soften cream cheese at room temperature. Drain chicken and add with bacon and seasoning.

Spread mixture on each tortilla. Roll up, wrap in plastic wrap and refrigerate for at least 1 hour.

When ready to serve, un-wrap and slice into one inch slices.

Have additional salsa available for those who have a spicy hankering.

CHICKEN SKEWER APPETIZERS

One chicken breast for each guest.

2   Tbs **Baja Adobo** seasoning
4   Tbs olive oil
2   Tbs Aleppo pepper
    Bamboo skewers

Slice boneless/skinless chicken breasts (usually 1 breast per guest) into ½ inch thick slices. Place on paper towel and dry both sides.

Place bamboo skewers in water for about 30 minutes. Combine ingredients in bowl and drag chicken through to coat well. Lay aside to dry for 10 minutes.

Skewer the chicken in a ripple manner and place on grill for about 3 minutes each side.

CHICKEN WRAPS SOUTHWEST STYLE

2   Tbs olive oil
2   Boneless chicken breasts cut into
     finger-sized slices
1   Medium onion, sliced
½   Tsp **Baja Adobo** seasoning
1   Medium red bell pepper
1   10¾-oz can mushroom soup
½   Cup Chunky salsa
1-2 Cups grated Mozzarella cheese
     Flour tortillas

Heat oil in skillet; add chicken, onion, **Baja Adobo** and Pepper. Cook until chicken is done and lightly browned. Add soup and salsa.

Cook until liquid is reduced by half. Spread on flour tortillas, sprinkle with cheese and fold over to serve.

CHIPOTLE SALSA

1   7-oz can Chipotle peppers in Adobo Sauce
½   Cup chopped cilantro
1   15¼ -oz jar Pace chunky salsa
1   Small onion, chopped
1   15¼-oz can corn, drained
1   15¼-oz black beans with juice

Put Chipotles in blender and blend until smooth. Mix other ingredients in a serving bowl. Add Chipotles. Mix and serve.

CRAB & CREAM CHEESE SPREAD

2   8-oz packages of cream cheese
1   Small onion, grated
2   Tbs chopped garlic
1   Tbs Worcestershire sauce
1   Tbs lemon juice
2   Tbs mayonnaise
1   Bottle chili sauce
2   4-oz cans minced crab, drained

Mix together well cream cheese, onion, garlic, Worcestershire sauce, lemon juice and mayonnaise. Spread mixture on platter. Spread chili sauce over mixture then pat crab meat over top.

CRAB DIP

1   4-oz can crab meat
1   Large package cream cheese
1½ Tsp Worcestershire sauce
½   Tsp **Baja Adobo** seasoning
2   Tsp lemon juice
1   Tsp minced garlic
    A dash of pepper sauce to taste.

Put all together and moisten with milk to desired consistency. Let set in refrigerator for at least one hour before serving.

CREAMY FRANKS

1   Lb cocktail franks
1   Cup sour cream
¼   Cup prepared yellow mustard

Mix together sour cream and mustard. Drain and add frankfurters. Bake in oven-proof dish for 20 minutes at 425°.

DEVILED EGGS

12 Eggs, boiled
¼ Cup Honey Mustard
¼ Cup spicy bread & butter pickles, chopped
¼ Cup onion, chopped
½ Tbs celery salt
2 Tbs apple cider vinegar
3 Slices bacon, fried crisp and crumbled

Place eggs in pan in cold water and turn on heat. When water has begun boiling, remove from burner and cover.

In large bowl mix together well all other ingredients. When eggs have cooled down, shell them and put yolks into bowl with other ingredients. Add additional honey mustard if necessary to obtain right consistency. Mix well and spoon into egg white centers.

FAUX GUACAMOLE

1 Package frozen peas, cooked and drained
1 Ripe avocado, peeled and cubed
½ Cup sour cream
¼ Cup chopped green onions
2 Tbs chopped cilantro
2 Tbs lime juice
½ Whole jalapeno, seeded and coarsely chopped

1   Small clove garlic, halved

1   Tsp **Baja Adobo** seasoning

Place all ingredients in a food processor. Process until smooth. Cover well. Refrigerate, overnight if desired.

This concoction will keep its green color much longer than real Guacamole.

Jalapeno Crab Dip

1   4-oz can crab meat

1   Tsp hot sauce

½   Tsp **Baja Adobo** seasoning

½   Cup mayonnaise

½   Cup finely chopped jalapeno peppers

¼   Lb. Monterey Jack cheese, with jalapeño, grated

1   6-oz package grated Asiago cheese

1   Tsp minced garlic

1   Tsp Worcestershire sauce

Preheat oven to 350°. Combine all but Asiago cheese in a medium-size mixing bowl. Toss gently to mix.

Spread in medium-size shallow baking dish. Sprinkle Asiago cheese evenly on top and bake for 25 minutes. Serve with crackers or chips.

In the Early Days...

...of ***Dr. Douglas' Wonder Bakers®,*** I traveled across the country, from Cheyenne, Wyoming to Roswell, New Mexico; from Galveston, Texas to Chicago, Illinois; From Ft. Dix, New Jersey down the East Coast to Melbourne, Florida, and most every large city in-between.

I traveled in a large van, carrying a cooking unit I had built. In each town I demonstrated the "Bakers". In family gourmet stores and in large department stores, I displayed my wares. In 1981, I put over 87,000 miles on that van.   I cooked during the day, and then traveled at night to the next town where I set up the Demo Unit and cooked again.

I usually left later than I should have, since I did not relish the long drives. On the drive to Ft. Dix, I tell the story that I *"swam all the way to New Jersey."* I drove straight through in my bathing suit. When I got sleepy or tired or both, I pulled into the parking area at the best motel and went swimming.

It became a tradition that when I returned I would stop at my favorite Mexican Food Restaurant, the ***"Villa Placita"*** in North Dallas.

There I would order a large margarita and a plate of nachos. I had eaten there over the years and working together with one of the owners, had helped them create the best Nacho meat that ever existed, *adding a little of this and a little of that*, until it had exactly the perfect combination of flavors.

Finally I got off the road and onto QVC. Some time during that time the Villa Placita sold to others and they changed everything. Including the name and the recipe for Nachos.

Several years ago, after trying them at every Mexican restaurant I visited, I decided to re-create the recipe, and began experimenting until I got it **RIGHT!**

AND HERE IT IS.

The recipe makes a lot of nacho meat, but you can freeze it in 2-cup portions. Then when you are ready for nachos—you got' um.

MACHO NACHOS

3   Lb ground beef
1   Lb ground pork
4   Tbs black pepper
4   Tbs minced garlic
2   Cups chopped onion
10 Tbs cumin
2   Tbs **Baja Adobo** seasoning
1   Cup mozzarella cheese, grated
1   Cup cheddar cheese, grated

Brown beef and pork; add onion and cook until the onions clear and meat is well-done and crumbly. Add other ingredients. Combine, cover and simmer about 20 minutes. Drain grease off.

Cover bottom of baking dish with whole chips.

Mix together mozzarella and cheddar cheese. Cover chips with half of the cheese. (Kraft's 5 cheese mix also works great).

Cover with one cup meat mixture.

Crush some more chips and spread evenly over top of meat.

Spread another cup of the meat mixture over crushed chips. Top with remaining cheese.

Add sliced jalapenos if you like and bake about 20 minutes at 425° or until cheese is well melted.

Use amount equal to how large a group you are feeding and then freeze the rest for later.

I like them like this because they are much easier than spooning the meat onto individual tortilla chips, so you can eat more, faster.

But if you like the traditional way, be my guest.

PARSLEY DIP

1	Bunch parsley
2	Cups onion
3	Cups red bell pepper

Use just the leaves from the parsley and process in food processor with the onion and red bell pepper until fine. Pour into large bowl.

ADD

4	Tbs chopped garlic	2	Tsp **Deep South Soul**
2	Tsp celery salt	2	Tbs olive oil
5	Drops sesame oil		

Stir well and let sit for a couple hours at room temperature before serving on pumpernickel bread.

QUESO FLAMEADO

(The recipe for Chorizo is under Pork Dishes.)

Put one patty in a skillet. Crumble and cook until completely done.

Grate two cups each of cheddar, mozzarella and Monterrey Jack into a bowl. Mix well.

Spread the Chorizo evenly in an oven-proof glass dish, cover with the cheese. Microwave until the cheese is well melted and bubbly.

Place on hot pads, being careful to keep well away from flammable materials or items.

Pour 1 jigger of (at least) 100 proof vodka into dish, light with barbeque lighter, (being careful not to burn your hand), mix well with long handled spoon and fork while the flame lasts.

Spread evenly and completely on flour tortillas, roll, slice and serve. Eat while hot.

SALSA SUPREME

4 Cloves garlic

8 Stalks cilantro

4 Roma tomatoes

1 Jalapeno

1 Tbs lime juice

¼ Cup green bell pepper

1 Tbs Baja Adobo

½ Large onion

Chop all vegetables finely, add lime juice and Baja Adobo.

Refrigerate for an hour. For a new taste, add ¼ of a medium cucumber, chopped.

SALSA VERDE

6	Tomatillos	6	Serrano peppers
1	Anaheim pepper	½	Cup white onion
6	Stalks cilantro	2	Tbs olive oil
2	Tsp **Baja Adobo** seasoning		

In medium pan bring 4 cups water to boil.

De-husk Tomatillos and put into boiling water. Add Serrano and Anaheim pepper. Simmer gently for 20 minutes. Remove from water.

Chop cilantro and white onion into pieces. Put peppers, Tomatillos, onion and cilantro into blender with **Baja Adobo** seasoning. Blend well.

In medium pan warm olive oil, add blender contents and simmer for 8 to 10 minutes until light boil is reached. Pour over enchiladas and enjoy.

Sausage Balls

2   Pounds hot sausage
2   Cups all-purpose baking mix
2   Cups grated sharp cheddar cheese
½   Cup chopped red bell pepper
½   Cup finely chopped onion

Combine all ingredients in large bowl and stir well. Form 1" balls. Place on un-greased baking sheet. Bake at 250° for 20 minutes or until golden brown.

Sausage Dip

1   Lb hot breakfast sausage
1   Lb hamburger meat
½   10¾ can cream of mushroom soup
1   Lb Velveeta cheese
1   Cup Pace's medium Picante sauce

Cook sausage and hamburger meat, stirring until meat forms fine crumbles. Drain well. Add soup, Picante and cheese. Heat and stir until cheese is melted and all ingredients are combined. Serve with corn chips.

CAUTION! This one is addictive.

SHRIMP QUESO DIP

1	Tbs butter
½	Lb shrimp, chopped
½	Tbs chopped garlic
1	Tbs **Deep South Soul** seasoning
1	Lb Queso cheese dip

Melt butter in skillet and sauté shrimp with garlic.
Add Deep South Soul and Queso cheese dip and warm over low heat.

SPINACH DIP

1	Pkg frozen spinach, chopped, thawed, drained
1	Cup mayonnaise
1	Cup sour cream
1	5-oz can water chestnuts, chopped
1	Pkg Knorr vegetable dry soup mix

Mix all ingredients together. Refrigerate over night for best flavor.

Tejun Caviar

15-oz can field peas, drained
1   Large green pepper, chopped
1   Large onion, chopped
1   10-oz can Ro-Tel tomatoes, medium heat
1   Tsp **Tejun** seasoning
1   Tbs **Baja Adobo** seasoning
1   Bunch cilantro, stems removed, chopped
½   Cup Spicy Italian dressing

Put all together, stir well, cover and set in refrigerator for at least 12 hours before serving.

Wings—Hot & Quick

18   Chicken wings
1   8-oz bottle French dressing
¼   Cup soy sauce
2   Tsp minced ginger

Combine dressing, soy sauce and ginger. Pour over chicken and marinate in refrigerator for several hours or over night. Place wings in oven-proof dish. Broil 10 minutes.

Turn once, brush with marinade and broil another 10 minutes.

BEEF DISHES

BEEF FAJITAS

In a medium pot—combine:

½ Cup each of: ¼ Cup each of:

Taylor New York Lake   Lemon juice
Country White wine   Lime juice
Pineapple juice   Orange juice
Soy sauce   Olive oil

ADD:

2   Tbs **New Mexico Chipotle** seasoning

1 Tbs each:

Garlic powder   Garlic chopped
New Mexico Chipotle   **Baja Adobo** seasoning
Black pepper

ADD: Zested peel of one orange and one lemon.

    Place on high heat and bring to a boil. Remove from heat and stir until oil is combined.

    Place 2 "Well trimmed" skirt steaks, about 2 Lbs each, into marinade. Marinate 2 hours at room temperature, turning every 30 minutes.

Remove from marinade and strip membrane from meat. Grill over high heat for 6 to 10 minutes.

Cut across grain into finger-length strips. Serve on flour tortillas with Salsa.

CHILI—NEARLY WORLD FAMOUS

1   Lb bacon

3   Lbs tenderized round steak

2   Large onions, chopped

3   Lbs lean ground chuck

4   Tbs minced garlic

3   46-oz cans tomato juice

2   Tbs black pepper

1   Tbs **Deep South Soul** seasoning

Fry bacon until very crisp, but not burned. (Use bacon in a sandwich or for potato salad). Put the grease into a 12 quart or larger stock pot.

Cut round steak in 1" chunks and place in stockpot, add ground chuck, black pepper, **Soul,** and brown all. Add onions and cook until clear.

Let simmer 30 minutes until thick roux develops. Add garlic and one can tomato juice, bring to boil, then turn heat down and simmer for 30 minutes.

ADD:

2	Tbs light brown sugar	4	Tbs cumin
4	Tbs olive oil	12	4-oz cans green
2	Whole jalapeno peppers		chilies, chopped
2	Tbs cayenne pepper	2	28-oz cans
3	Tbs chili powder		crushed tomatoes
1	Tsp Chile Arbol	3	27-oz cans tomato
3	Tbs ground sage		soup
3	Tbs lemon juice	3	Tbs ground oregano
2	Tbs **New Mexico Chipotle**		
2	Tbs **Baja Adobo** seasoning		

Add remaining two cans tomato juice and cook at ***low boil*** for 2 hours, stirring often. If too thin, add *"Masa flour"* 1 Tbs at a time. Let set overnight at room temperature before serving.

CHILI SQUASH

1	Tsp olive oil
2	Cups sliced yellow summer squash
1	Tbs **Deep South Soul** seasoning
½	Cup whole kernel corn,
¼	Cup grated Monterrey Jack cheese
¾	Cup chopped onion
2	4-oz cans whole green chilies, drained
2	Tbs apple cider vinegar
⅛	Tsp red pepper sauce

Sauté onions in oil. Add squash; stir, cover, reduce heat and cook until tender. Pour into baking dish. Slice chilies into strips. Layer over squash.

Combine corn, salt, red pepper sauce and wine. Spread over chilies. Bake at 425° for 15 minutes. Take out, top with cheese and bake another 6 minutes.

BRISKET IN CHIPOTLE-ONION SAUCE

2   Tbs minced garlic
2   Tbs light brown sugar
1   Tbs ground cumin
1   Tsp **Baja Adobo** seasoning
2½ Cups sliced onions
1   4-5 pound beef brisket, trimmed well
1   Cup chili sauce
1   7-oz cans chipotles in Baja Adobo sauce

Spread half of onions on bottom of baking dish lined with heavy duty aluminum foil. Place brisket in pan.

Combine garlic, brown sugar, cumin and **Baja Adobo**. Sprinkle well over top of brisket. Place remainder of onions on top of meat.

Puree chili sauce with chipotles and spread over meat and onions.

Close foil tightly around meat. Place in oven in the evening. Set the temperature of oven at lowest setting and cook overnight.

Remove meat. Put liquid and onions in sauce-pan and cook until reduced. Place in blender and cream to serve with meat.

GYROS

1	Lb ground lamb	4	Tbs minced garlic
1	Lb ground lean beef	½	Tsp ground Fenugreek
4	Slices day-old white bread	2	Tbs **Santorini** seasoning
½	Tbs ground cumin	4	Tbs fresh parsley (chopped fine)
2	Tbs fine dill weed		
2	Tbs **Baja Adobo** seasoning	½	Tsp ground black pepper
2	Eggs, beaten		

Mix lamb and beef together well. Crumble bread into mixture and mix well.

Combine and mix well all spices. Add to meat. Add eggs and mix well. Form into log about 2" in diameter. Wrap in aluminum foil. Let set in refrigerator for at least four hours. Bake in 300° oven for 1½ hours, Slice and serve on pita bread with Tzatziki Sauce, recipe follows.

TZATZIKI SAUCE

2	Cups plain Yogurt. (Santorini yogurt is best.)
2	Tbs olive oil
4	Tbs finely minced garlic,
1	Tbs **Santorini** seasoning

1   Tbs lemon juice

½   Tsp **Baja Adobo** seasoning

2   Tbs fresh dill, chopped finely

1   Medium cucumber, washed, seeded. With skin.

Place cloth over bowl and drain yogurt (If using pre-stirred yogurt, skip.) for about an hour. Combine yogurt, olive oil, garlic, Santorini seasoning, lemon juice, and **Baja Adobo** in a bowl. Cover and let set for one hour.

Shred cucumber, then squeeze by hand until liquid is gone. Add cucumber and dill to yogurt mixture. Mix well.

MEAT LOAF ON THE GRILL

2   Yellow onions, diced finely

1½ Lbs. lean ground beef

     Cup tomato paste

½   Cup dry bread crumbs

1-2 Cups grated white cheddar cheese

¼   Cut fresh parsley leaves, roughly chopped

1   Egg, beaten

3   Tsp course ground black pepper

3   Tsp Kosher salt, divided

½   Lb. new potatoes cut into 1 inch chunks

4   Tbs olive oil

Heat grill to medium. Finely dice 1 onion, In large bowl, combine; onions, beef, tomato paste, bread crumbs, cheese, parsley, egg, 1 Tsp black pepper and 2 Tsp salt.

Place 2 sheets foil, each 3' long, stacked on top of each other. Fold the foil in half so there's a crease in the center. Coat the top piece of foil lightly with oil to keep from sticking.

Place mixture in center of right half and mold into loaf. Cut one onion in 1" wedges and place around loaf. Season loaf with remaining salt and pepper.

Fold the left side of foil over the top and fold all edges together to seal tightly.

Place on grill and cook, turning upside down every 6-7 seven minutes until cooked thru (150° 0n instant read thermometer) approximately 40 minutes.

MEAT LOAF SUPREME

2   Cups crushed saltines

½   Cup onion flakes

2   Eggs, slightly mixed with fork

3   Lbs ground chuck or other lean beef

2½ Tsp **Deep South Soul** seasoning

1   Tsp dry mustard

¼   Cup milk

¼   Cup catsup

Preheat oven to 400°.

Mix crackers, onions, eggs and meat, tossing lightly as possible. Add all other ingredients. Mix thoroughly but as lightly as possible.

Put into 9" x 9" baking dish and bake 30 minutes.

TOPPING:

¼   Cup brown sugar
¼   Cup prepared mustard
½   Cup Catsup

Mix well and spread over meat loaf. Return to oven and cook 20 more minutes.

MEAT LOAF—NEW MEXICO STYLE

1½ Pounds ground beef
1   Cup Pace Picante sauce
1   8-oz can tomato sauce
8   Pimento-stuffed olives
1   Tbs **New Mexico Chipotle** seasoning
⅓   Cup oats
1   Egg
¼   Tsp pepper
½   Cup chopped onion

Mix thoroughly ½ of the tomato sauce and all ingredients except olives.

Make loaf and place in loaf pan.

Spread remaining tomato sauce over top and push olives just into loaf.

Bake at 350° for 55 minutes.

TACO PIE

¼   Lb lean ground beef

½   Cup Chopped onion

1   Envelope taco seasoning

1   4-oz can chopped green chilies

1   Egg

¼   Cup milk

¼   Cup biscuit mix

¼   Cup grated cheddar cheese

Brown onions, drain. Add seasoning, spread evenly in 9" baking dish. Spread chilies on top. Beat egg, add milk and biscuit mix. Stir well and spread on top of chilies. Bake at 400° for 15 minutes.

Top with cheese and bake for another 7 minutes.

TAMALE PIE

CRUST:

4½ Cups water in pot
2   Tsp chili powder
2   Tsp **Deep South Soul** seasoning
2½ Cups yellow cornmeal

Combine all and cook until thick consistency is reached. Line the bottom and sides of a baking dish with half of the mixture.

FILLING:

2   Tbs oil
1   Lb lean ground beef
2   Tbs **New Mexico Chipotle** seasoning
1   Chopped green bell pepper
1   Cup chopped onion
2   Tbs chopped garlic
1   15¼-oz can cream-style corn
2   Stalks celery, finely chopped
1   14¾-oz can chopped tomatoes, drained

Simmer mixture over medium heat, stirring often until it thickens. Pour over crust in baking dish and cover with remaining crust mixture.

Sprinkle 1 cup of grated Muenster cheese over top. Bake at 350° for 45 minutes.

West Coast Hamburgers

2   Lbs lean ground chuck
1   Cup chopped onion
3   Tbs soy sauce
3   Anaheim peppers, chopped
6   Slices Monterrey Jack cheese
2   Avocados, halved, pitted, peeled, and thinly
    sliced

Roast pepper in oven or on grill until skin is blistered. Put in paper sack and seal until cool enough to handle. Take out and remove skin, stem and seeds. Chop finely.

Combine beef, onion, soy sauce and peppers in a large mixing bowl; add beef and mix well. Shape mixture into 4 patties about 1 inch thick.

Place patties on grill directly over medium heat. Grill for 15 to 20 minutes turning burgers once halfway through grilling. Top with cheese slices and sliced avocados for the last 5 minutes of grilling.

Serve with condiments your family or guests like.

SPICES

There are spices mentioned that you may not be familiar with. Information on the spices mentioned in this book can be found by visiting our website at www.downhomespices.com

Aleppo and Fenugreek are available at most oriental spice stores or in a spice catalog.

A Rabbit on the Roof

I took a trip across the waves,
To England I did travel,
I enjoyed it till I called home,
Then things began to unravel.

My brother answered the phone
And asked how I was doing,
I replied that it was great,
Unprepared for the story ensuing.

When I asked about my dog,
My brother quickly replied,
"Old Ben ran out in the road,
A truck hit and he died."

Let me stop right here and tell you this,
That dog was my best friend.
Together we chased many a rabbit
And on him I could always depend.

It is an understatement
To say the shock was great.
I'd had him since he was a pup
And just last year he was eight.

My sadness was most real
And my anguish was profound.
Had my brother been in front of me,
I'd have knocked him to the ground.

"Why did you have to tell me that way?
Why were you not gentle instead?"
"Wouldn't made any difference," said he,
"Old Ben would still be dead."

"That's not what I mean," I cried,
"I mean tell me in a different way."
"Well, if you're so smart," he tersely said,
"Just what would you have had me say?"

"It's not hard to just be kind,
You can always make up a story.
Then when you have to break bad news,
It won't sound quite so gory."

"You could've said, that the other day,
You and Ben were just being lazy,
When a rabbit ran across the roof,
And old Ben just plain went crazy."

"He ran up the stairs, and onto the roof,
And around and around they went.
When he caught the rabbit, he fell off,
Cause his strength had all been spent."

"I would have then felt better,
For I'd know old Ben died happy."
"Well, OK," my brother said,
But to me that sounds plum sappy."

"And how would a rabbit get on the roof,
Is something I'd like to ask?"
My brother's never been considered bright
So I began to take him to task.

"It doesn't matter how it got on the roof,
Try to use your imagination."
Then I just quit and hung up the phone,
Talking more would've ruined my vacation.

I continued on my travels,
There was nothing else I could do.
My brother never would understand,
About being kind he hadn't a clue.

From some small town in France,
I decided to make another call.
I really didn't want to talk to him,
But he's my brother after all.

"What things are going on over there?"
I asked, trying hard not to sound aloof.
"Not a lot," he said, "But yesterday,
Grandma saw a rabbit on the roof."

THE BALLAD OF JAKE LEAMON

Jake Leamon was a fine carpenter,
Who lived in the land down under.
And the day he made a life changing move,
It gave all of his friends cause to wonder.

He was a craftsman of wood without peer,
He could build what you wanted to your liking,
He had an exceptional eye for detail,
And the result would always be striking.

His reputation was known far and wide,
Though he charged the highest of prices.
You could take his word to do what he said,
And he had no Interrupting vices.

People came to him for the value,
They knew for sure they would receive.
And when received their order,
They never had cause to grieve.

But Jake had a dream in his heart,
That would not let go of his mind,
He wanted to travel a different path,
Where someday his destiny he'd find.

Then one day a stranger came by,
And a wondrous story he told.
He had just come from the USA,
And had pockets full of pure gold.

"Why the gold there is everywhere,
Just waiting for the next lucky man.
You can walk out; pick up all your want,
By just reaching out your hand."

The story the stranger related,
Was passed off as just a wild tale,
But others came and the stories they told,
Were on a much grander scale.

"One of these days this work I'll lay down,
And have a go at this treasure."
Jake might have gone at that very time,
Had his wife not expressed her displeasure.

And the USA was a long way off,
To get there took a long time.
So back to his work, Jake reluctantly went,
Even though he was passing his prime.

Then word came about gold to be had,
In a place that was not too far off.
So Jake vowed to not miss this chance,
Though his friends at him did all scoff.

"What makes you want to waste your life,
On such a hopeless wild dream?"
But Jake knew if he didn't give it a go,
He'd lose all his own self-esteem.

So he sold his shop and his lumber,
And all of his carpenter's tools,
Only kept what he knew would be needed,
And joined in on a journey with fools.

He caught a train to the end of the line,
And there bought himself an old mule.
Everyone knew there, by his skin so fair,
Here was another foolish, dreaming fool.

But Jake was determined, wouldn't turn back
And on his journey he did travel,
The trip was long; his food most ran out,
Before he got to the gold-bearing gravel.

He worked long, though little did he find,
But his spirit never did break.
Selling his tools, with the little he found,
He finally had a new stake.

Wherever he went, he was always too late,
And when his tools were all gone,
And he had sold the old mule,
Jake finally resigned to his fate.

From the side of a hill near a creek,
He dug out a bunch of the clay.
Built a house, and when his food ran out,
He lay down, and Jack died where he lay.

If you go there today, it's a beautiful place,
The land is green as far as you can see.
Many grains grow there, three crops a year,
And sweet fruit grows on most every tree.

The land is so fertile, little work is required,
And the water is plentiful and clean.
Many animals are raised and are so well fed,
The meat is tender and lean.

But Jake missed it all, looked only for gold,
And his search clouded his vision,
Farming was not his way to get rich,
And farmers he considered with derision.

When other men came to level the ground,
Getting ready to plant the first crop,
Knocking over Jake's shack; on the bulldozer blade,
What they saw made the workers all stop.

When Jake dug the clay to build his hut,
That would become his last abode,
Had he dug a bit more, into the hill,
He'd have discovered the great mother lode.

From that hill they took more gold,
Than they had at the first.
But Jake missed out on the gold,
He would have said he was just cursed.

So when you're ready to quit,
Giving up a dream, You've had
As your reason for existence,
Remember Jake;
Give it one more good lick,

Nothing ever pays off like persistence.

THAT "B & B" CAT

How long has it been now? Six years? Seems hardly so long. Miss Jean and I had fulfilled a Christmas present I had given to her to spend a week in a Bed & Breakfast just about 4 miles north of Fredericksburg, Texas.

Quiet, out in the country, just off a Caliche rock road with a spring fed creek running just outside the back porch door, it was an idyllic place. Though there were other cabins on the property, there was no one else there. For the uninitiated, and those not familiar with the area, it is just about the middle of the *Texas Hill Country*, so named for the many hills in the country, I have to assume.

We checked in at the managing office in town then drove out and unpacked for a three day stay. We drove back into Fredericksburg for dinner then took a walk about the town, which, being as the hour was after seven pm, was already closed up. When we arrived back it was dark and peaceful and quiet and ideal for a much needed and appreciated getaway from daily activities. Then we had a visitor.

A long haired grey, white and black tabby cat was comfortably ensconced on the front porch totally blocking the screen door.

Now we are both lovers of cats and it was a delight that, when we finally moved him and opened the door, he took the lead in entering. Deliberately he walked to the kitchen area and sat in front of the refrigerator with an expectant air, as if to say, "OK, I'm here, I'm hungry, you're here to feed me, so what's the hesitation?"

Luckily we had brought leftovers from the restaurant, so we did not have to suffer whatever the consequences were if we could not have fed him. After he had carefully, and pickingly, eaten to his satisfaction, he sauntered into the bedroom, lay down under the end of the bed and went to sleep. This seeming to be a routine he had practiced often so when time to go to bed arrived, we left him there.

And, what a bed it was. It had an iron bedstead, quite high off the floor with the soft, feather bed-like feeling I had grown used to when I was growing up. It was in January, so the temperature called for ample covering, and there were quilts the like of which I had not slept under since the days of my youth. I lay down and crashed.

Some time in the middle of the night I awoke and in the process of rolling from my right side to my left side, felt a lump at my feet. It was the cat. He had curled himself into the crook of my foot and was sound asleep. Careful not to disturb him I continued my changing of sides and returned to my slumber.

When I awoke the next morning, he was gone from the end of the bed. When I went into the kitchen to turn up the thermostat and turn on the coffee, there he was, lying in front of the refrigerator with the same look of expectation I had encountered the night before. With the same results I might add.

As we continued our visit, he would greet us in the evening when we returned from our leisure tourist adventures, go to sleep under the bed, move to the bottom of the bed and against my legs sometime in the night, and then greet me at the refrigerator in the morning.

Where we first thought he was an abandoned cat who had found his way to our door, we came to realize by his routine that he was a fixture at the place, though we had seen no one come and go all the time we had been there. We began to purchase cat food and bring it back with us in the evening.

On the morning of our departure he took off out the door as usual. The previous evening I had backed the van in rather close to the door to facilitate the loading. When about finished I walked to the driver's side of the van to open the door, there he was sprawled out in front of the left front tire. When I reached down to pick him up, he actually grabbed the grass and held on to the point I had to pull rather hard to dislodge him.

As we were about to leave, Jean noticed a book on the table in front of the fireplace and opened it to find comments left by others. We were comforted to learn that the cat was a fixture at the place. As we were leaving we stopped by one of the outbuildings to find that what was once a chicken house had been converted to a cat condominium. Each of the boxes where the chickens used to lay eggs were now mostly beds for this cat that had captured the hearts and imaginations of many others who had been there before us.

Now I have always been a lover of cats, and upon our return to Dallas I suggested that we might think about getting a cat. All Jean would say is, "If we can find one like that, then…"

Would you believe it, in the Sunday paper section SPCA sponsors "Adopt a Cat" and there was a picture of a cat that looked to be the twin of the *"B & B Cat."* We had a trip to California scheduled for the next day and promised ourselves to go see if it was still there when we returned a week later.

Sure enough we went, and sure enough it was still there, and sure enough it looked just like the *"B &B Cat"* we had come to like.

Unfortunately…well that is another story.

BREAKFAST DISHES

Baked Egg Brunch

10 Eggs, beaten
1 Cup mayonnaise
2 Roma tomatoes, diced
½ Cup slivered ham or crumbled bacon
1 Pkg shredded mozzarella cheese
1 Cup milk
½ Cup chopped green onions, including tops
1 Tbs butter

Melt butter in oven-proof dish. Mix all ingredients together and pour into dish.

Bake at 350° for 25 minutes or middle is set.

Cheese Biscuits

2 Cups biscuit mix or self-rising flour
½ Cup grated cheddar cheese
½ Cup beer

Mix all together; beat vigorously until dough forms. On a floured board, knead five times. Roll dough into ½" thickness, cut with 2" biscuit cutter. Place on baking pan. Bake at 425° for 10-14 minutes.

Big Al's Deli in Plano, Texas

In 1980 I discovered Al Galmedi at his Deli in Plano, Texas and entered into a friendship that lasted for many years. Big Al was about the most interesting man I have ever met. He was born, raised and educated by Jewish parents in Egypt.

Before the war between Israel and Egypt in 1947 he and his parents moved to Israel where he served as an officer in the army on the staff of Moshe Dyan.

Later he moved to Greece. After a series of activities, he worked for and became the head chef of the Hilton Hotels.

When he retired, he moved to Plano and opened "Big Al's Deli" just off the square in the old downtown section.

Such food as he did prepare.

Never having been a fan of chicken livers, I declined them one day when they were the special. He ignored my order and brought them instead. Served over white rice with a sauce that was thick and brown, I went nuts over them.

I introduced many friends and business associates to the Deli. I ate there so often, I didn't bother to order as he would just bring me what he wanted me to have. Everything was incredible.

When he retired and closed the Deli, I felt I had lost a relative.

One dish I ate repeatedly for breakfast was Chouk Chuoka. It was made from the combination of many vegetables, wilted in a pot with olive oil…well the recipe follows.

One day I decided I would like to recreate the dish and remembered he had a sign posted in the store that named the vegetables it included.

I drove to Plano and looked in the window, hoping to be able to read it. Sadly, it was gone.

However, I was determined to recreate the recipe and began to experiment. The result follows.

CHOUK CHUOKA

2   Cups celery cut in ½" pieces

2   Anaheim peppers, cut into thin slices

1   Cup red onion chopped into ½" pieces

1   Cup green bell pepper chopped into ½" pieces

2   Bunches parsley, chopped

3   Cups cilantro, chopped

2   Just-ripe Roma tomatoes, chopped

½   Cup olive oil

1   Tbs celery salt

¼   Cup of Sauce (recipe below)

6-9 Eggs

Prepare vegetables as above and place in large pot or skillet with olive oil and celery salt. Sauté over medium heat until onions clear and parsley and cilantro wilt. Stir constantly.

Spread ¾" thick layer in large skillet. Break eggs into mixture. Cover and cook until egg whites turn solid but yokes are still runny.

CHOUK CHUOKA SAUCE

½ Cups chopped onion
½ Cup chopped green pepper
½ Cup olive oil
2 Cups Pace medium Picante sauce
4 Tbs chopped garlic
3 Fresh jalapenos, de-seeded, de-veined, chopped
2 Cups chopped cilantro
1 Anaheim pepper, de-seeded, de-veined, chopped

Place first three items in stew pan and cook until onions clear. Add other four ingredients and cook all until oil is fully combined and sauce thickens (about two hours.)

As a condiment or dip: excellent for sandwiches, pinto beans, all meats and even on baked potatoes.

HUEVOS Y FRIJOLES NEGROS

2 Cups black beans, cooked, drained, mashed
3 Tbs olive oil
2 Tbs crushed garlic
½ Cup chopped onion
1 Anaheim pepper, de-seeded, de-veined, chopped
1 Cup salsa
1 Cup shredded Monterrey Jack cheese

5-6 Flour tortillas
5-6 Eggs

Sauté garlic, onion and pepper in olive oil. Mash beans and add to mixture. Heat and stir until smooth.

Spread on tortilla. Fry each egg in olive oil and place on tortilla. Add salsa and cheese and serve.

FOOTBALL FRIENDS FOREVER

Bill and Joe were such good friends,
They were always side by side.
They trusted each other in every way,
And in each other did confide.

They worked, and played together,
And would each support the other.
If you ever met Bill you would swear,
That Joe had to be his brother.

Even as just boys, they were the same,
And had once even taken a vow,
They would be friends forever,
With loyalty, they did the other endow.

They liked every sport, played every one,
Their favorite being football.
They played in high school and in college,
And were always the heroes of fall.

Their passion remained after they grew up,
As they supported their alma maters.
Whey they grew older, and couldn't play,
They became dedicated spectators.

With football Friday and Saturday,
Then the pros on Sunday.
They could just not get enough,
And watched every game on Monday.

Said Bill one day, "What's gonna happen,
The time comes one of us dies?"
"If you go first," said Joe, "And no game is on,
I'll come and say my goodbyes."

"That's not what I mean, what will we do,
If there's no football in heaven?"
"It could be, not enough players make it,
That they can't get together eleven."

"I know what let's do
That will solve the situation."
"Whoever goes first, comes back,
And gives the other illumination."

So they agreed and took an oath,
And were bound to do the act.
Whoever went first, would find out,
And the other then contact.

One day Bill died, and with no game on,
Joe came to see his friend off.
Then once he had, he took his leave,
And played eighteen holes of golf.

Then one dark night, Joe heard a voice,
That filled his heart with dread.
There, plain as could be, he saw Bill,
Standing at the foot of his bed.

"You did it old friend, you made it back,
What news do you bring for me?"
"Is there football there, do we play,
Or watch? Don't keep me in agony."

"The news is," said Bill, "There is football,
Twenty- four hours a day."
"And oh, there is such glorious field,
We watch and even get to play."

"Go ahead and tell me all," Said Joe,
"Don't keep me in suspense."
"Well," Bill said, "At tomorrow's game,
You're on the starting defense."

MY LIFE THIS YEAR

As I considered
My life this year,
Of all the people
I hold dear,
Right at the top,
There is you.

There've been times
That were easy,
There've been times
That were queasy,
Times that were happy,
Times that were blue.

Challenges came by
And left their mark,
But never once
Did I walk in the dark,
For the joy you brought
Brightened every day.

In all of the ups,
And all of the downs,
In all of the smiles
And all of the frowns,
You strengthened me,
Helped me find my way.

CHICKEN DISHES

Chicken Casserole

1   Lb. boneless skinless chicken, diced
½   Cup diced onion
1   Tsp salt
2   Tsp **Baja Adobo** seasoning
2   Tsp garlic salt
1   14½-oz diced tomatoes with green chilies,
    drained
2   Cups shredded cheddar cheese
3   Ounces cream cheese,
1   Cup sour cream

In deep skillet, simmer chicken breasts and onion in 1 cup filtered water with salt, pepper, garlic salt and **Baja Adobo**. Cook until chicken is no longer pink. Let cool and cut into ½ cubes.

Place chicken on the bottom of a baking dish with ¼ Tsp melted butter. Cover with tomatoes and a thin layer of cheddar cheese.

Next cover with cream cheese then sour cream. Top with remaining cheddar cheese.

Bake for 20 minutes or until cheese is thoroughly melted and ingredients are combined.

Chicken Enchiladas Especial

2 Medium chicken breasts

½ Cup chopped onion

2 Tsp **Baja Adobo** seasoning

2 Chicken bouillon cubes

3 Tbs olive oil

6 Flour tortillas

½ Cup sour cream

1 Cup grated Monterrey Jack cheese

Bring 4 cups water to boil, add chicken, onion, salt and bouillon. Cover and simmer 40 minutes or until chicken is tender.

Remove chicken and allow to cool. Cut chicken into small to medium strips. Heat oil until fairly hot. Carefully dip each side in oil for about 2 seconds, coating completely.

Fill tortillas with chicken; sprinkle each with grated cheese and fold over. Place in preheated 9" x 9" oven-proof baking dish.

Cover evenly with green chili sauce and put sour cream in strip down middle. Bake at 300° for 10 minutes.

Chicken Supreme

1 Cup cooked rice

½ Cup chopped celery

1 10-oz pkg frozen broccoli

2   Cups bite size cooked chicken
1   10¾-oz can cream of mushroom soup
½   Cup grated cheddar cheese
½   Cup cashews, chopped

In baking dish layer rice, followed by celery, broccoli, chicken and soup. Top with cheese. Sprinkle with cashews. Bake at 350° for 25 minutes.

DEEP SOUTH CHICKEN

1   Large chicken breast
2   Tsp **Deep South Soul** seasoning
4   Slices bacon

Place 2 slices bacon in 9" baking dish, place chicken breasts on top.
Place 2 slices bacon on top.
Sprinkle **Deep South Soul** evenly over all.
Bake for 12 minutes at 425°.

ORANGE-ONION CHICKEN

8   Drumsticks or thighs
1   Package Lipton's onion soup mix
1   8-oz frozen orange juice

Thaw the orange juice and add the Onion Soup mix and stir well.

Dip chicken in mix and layer baking dish. Bake in 425° oven for 18 minutes.

Use the remainder of the marinade to baste the chicken as it cooks.

PechuGas de Pollo Con Quail Sauce

STEP 1

In small pan, bring to boil 1 cup of water. Add:

¼   Cup chopped onion,

2   Chicken bouillon cubes,

¼   Tsp **Baja Adobo** seasoning

1   Cup Orzo pasta.

Cover and stir frequently until all water is absorbed.

3-4 Skinless chicken breasts, sliced into 1" strips, dust with **Baja Adobo** seasoning and marinate 2 hours in the refrigerator.

¼   Lb. bacon. Chop into ½" pieces and fry until almost crisp. Set aside.

½   Cup toasted Pinion nuts

STEP 2

TO ABOUT ¼ CUP BACON GREASE ADD:

¼   Cup of olive oil

2   Tbs chopped garlic

½   Tsp cumin

1   Cup chopped onion

2   Tbs butter

Cook until onion clears. Add chicken to sauce and cover. Cook on MEDIUM to HIGH heat for about 5 minutes on each side. Let chicken take on a light brown color.

ADD:

1   Anaheim pepper cut into thin rings.
1   Cup chopped cilantro.
1   Cup Taylor's Lake Country White wine.

Add cooked Orzo. Simmer another 5 minutes, stirring constantly until sauce thickens. Add bacon and toasted Pinion nuts. Serve with asparagus.

TAJUN STYLE CHICKEN

2   Large chicken breasts
2   Tsp **Tajun** seasoning
2   Strips bacon

Place chicken in 9" x 9" baking dish. Cut bacon in half and crisscross over each breast. Sprinkle **Tajun** seasoning evenly over breasts.

Bake at 435° for 20 minutes.

I Wanna Be an Angel When I Die

I've read many stories,
In the Record they are told.
How angels walked upon the earth,
And worked in days of old.

To some they brought good news,
To others they brought bad.
To kings they brought destruction,
To peasants, tidings glad.

It seems they were a busy bunch,
As about the earth they flew.
Helping here, hindering there,
As the whole of mankind grew.
I wanna be an angel,
When it comes my time to die.
I'll travel all around the world,
For then I'll surely fly.

To other worlds, perhaps I'll go,
For then they'll not be far.
For an angel it's no trick,
To reach out and touch a star.

To those who are in trouble,
I'll bring good news to them.
To help them through their trials,
Their flood of problems stem.

To all the little children,
Who huddle in their fright.
I'll let them know someone's there,
To help them through the night.

To those who are in sorrow,
I'll gently touch their hand.
Whisper kind words to their hearts,
To help them understand.

To those who stumble as they go,
Unable to find their way,
I'll lift them up, and steady them,
Help them make it through each day.

To everyone who is alone,
I'll sit and listen to them talk.
To those going down a long dark path,
I'll join them as they walk.

To those weighted down with burdens,
I'll quietly give a lift,
To separated lovers,
I'll help them heal the rift.

I'll be off on a grand adventure,
Bid me no sad goodbye.
For to leave this world brings me no fear,
For I'm gonna be an angel when I die.

"PYWAKIT"

So…here we are at the SPCA looking at a copy of the "B & B" cat. Alas though, it did not have the same temperament and was much older. While Jean was in the process of deciding if she *really* wanted it, I went into the *"come on in and spend a little time playing with our cats and you are sunk"* area.

As I leisurely walked around, a beautifully marked Calico cat got up from her nap on a shoulder high walkway and came over to me, talking and smoozing up to me in the most sensuous way.

Here I must confess that I have always loved Calico cats. I have no idea why or when it started, but they have always been my favorite kind of cat, and this young lady was absolutely beautiful. And the way she moved right into my arms when I reached out to her took my heart.

I glanced up to see Jean coming from the direction where she had been visiting with the other cat. I spoke quickly as I put her down. "See the lady coming there? Go over and work your magic on her and we'll take you home with us today."

When Jean entered the visiting room, the Calico went straight to her and wound herself around Jeans legs, and as Jean bent to pick her up, I played the innocent.

When asked about the one we had come to see, Jean said she thought he was too old and not really friendly. All this time the Calico was smoozing up to Jean and Jean was petting and rubbing her.

"What about this one," Jean asked.

"Certainly is pretty and seems to be loving," I replied with an air of feigned detachment.

The ruse worked perfectly, and after completing all the papers we were on the way home with a new pet. When we got her into the car, we became acquainted with a sound we have become accustomed to hearing when we take her in the car anywhere. And so she assumed her name.

I have a favorite Christmas movie. It is really not a Christmas movie but the story does take place during Christmas time and I watch it every December as it puts me in the Christmas mood. It stars Jimmy Stewart, Kim Novak, Jack Lemmon, Ernie Kovak and a number of other well known actors.

If you have never seen it, it is "Bell, Book and Candle," and is a delightful story, character, dialogue driven movie that I never get tired of watching. Jimmy plays a book publisher, Kim plays a witch, Jack plays a warlock and Ernie plays a writer of books on witchcraft and the interaction is hilarious.

Kim's character had a seal-point Siamese cat she used as a medium and the cat had a cry that permeates the mind. This is the sound which the new cat in our lives made and thus this beautiful young lady's name became *"Pywakit."*

When we brought *Pywakit* into the house she immediately set out upon a tour to see if it met her needs and made it into every room before she came back into the kitchen and set herself in front of the refrigerator, looking at us with the expectation of being fed. And so she was.

For the first, oh…about ten nights, she made her bed with us, making sure she was touching one or the other of us, then, once she had established herself as the queen of the domicile, she has since then slept everywhere except with us. But she still climbs into my lap occasionally to give me a little of her affection.

We had decided to keep her inside all the time because of the wild animals that occasionally roam the neighborhood. (Yes, even in the middle of Dallas there are opossums, raccoons and the occasional coyote that comes up from White Rock Creek which runs about four blocks away.)

But she would look so longingly out the windows of the garden room I decided to undertake what Jean (and others I told about my venture) said was not possible. I was going to train *Pywakit* to walk with me on a leash.

It was really not much of a problem putting the halter on the first time, but when it came to getting her to follow me; well for about three days when I would tell Jean I was taking *Pywakit* outside I referred to it as "taking my cat for a drag."

She would just simply fall on her side and remain there, complaining all the time. So I would drag her a little way, pick her up and put her on her feet and start all over again, with the same results.

Believe it or not, within a short time, she was walking on the leash and I would follow. All over the back yard she would lead me, smelling and examining everything along the way. After about two weeks of walking at least one time a day, I un-hooked the leash and as we walked she would remain the same distance as the leash had allowed. It was great!

Of course this led to letting her outside without me and then trying to keep her in the back yard. I put in a driveway gate with a gate opener and some screening across the back of the fence with the intention of keeping her in the back yard. Yeah sure.

When I would find her in the front of the house I would pick her up, hold her close to my chest and step hard, jarring both of us, saying no, no, no, no! I would even paddle her bottom sometimes, telling her no, no, no!

Soon, when I would catch her in the front yard, as soon as she saw me, she would hi-tail it to the back of the house, into the garage and be waiting at the door to get in when I got there, tucking her head to avoid the punishment she thought was coming.

Today, we let her out when she wants and every so often through the day, she will inevitably be at one of the doors to check in to let us know she is OK and ready to come back into the house. And, to the amazement of everyone, when I go outside in the evening and whistle for her; wherever she is, she comes into the yard, into the garage and stands at the door letting us know she wants in with her special cry.

Another trick she had taught us is the elevator game. She has her access to the top of the house via the front fence and often goes there to observe the neighborhood from that vantage point. When she is ready to come down she comes to the back of the house and begins her special cry and I know she wants down. So I go into the garage, get the stepstool and her "elevator box" (a cardboard box I keep there for just that purpose,) and hold it up so she can climb in and lower her to the ground. Mind you now, she is NOT spoiled!

FAJITAS

Beef Fajitas

In a medium pot—combine:

½ Cup each of: ¼ Cup each of:

Taylor New York Lake   Lemon juice
Country White wine   Lime juice
Pineapple juice   Orange juice
Soy sauce   Olive oil

Add:

2   Tbs **New Mexico Chipotle** seasoning

1 Tbs each:

Garlic powder
Garlic chopped
New Mexico Chipotle
Baja Adobo seasoning
Black pepper

ADD: Zested peel of one orange and one lemon.

Place on high heat and bring to a boil. Remove from heat and stir until oil is combined.

Place 2 "Well trimmed" Skirt steaks, about 2 Lbs each, into marinade. Marinate 2 hours at room temperature, turning every 30 minutes.

Remove from marinade and strip membrane from meat. Grill over high heat for 6 to 10 minutes.

Cut across grain into finger-length strips. Serve on flour tortillas with Salsa.

CHICKEN FAJITAS

In a medium pot, combine:

¼ Cup soy sauce
2 Tbs garlic powder
⅛ Lb butter
½ Cup white wine (I use new York Lake Country)
2 Tbs olive oil
1 Tsp **Baja Adobo** seasoning
1 Tsp cumin

Bring to a boil, and stir until all is combined. Place up to four breasts in the marinade for one minute each. If the mixture loses its boil, bring back to a boil before placing the next breast in. Continue until all breasts have been blanched.

Place breasts in appropriate sized container and cover with marinade. Let marinate 2 hours at room temperature.

Grill on high heat for 6-8 minutes. Cut into finger-length strips.

Plan on one chicken breast for each person.

This is also great for shrimp and scallops.

FAJITA ONIONS

In a small pot, place 4 beef bouillon cubes in 2 cups water, bring to boil and let cubes dissolve.

ADD:

½ Cup white wine

½ Cup soy sauce

2 Tbs lemon juice

2 Tbs wine vinegar

4 Jalapeno peppers, stems & seeds removed, quartered

½ Tbs garlic powder

1 Tbs olive oil

2 Large onions

Peel and cut onions into ½ inch pieces. Add to mixture.

Marinate onions for 2 hours at room temperature. (Stir every thirty minutes to make sure all onions have been marinated.

Heat skillet on medium setting and add 2 Tbs butter and ¼ cup marinade. Add onions and peppers and cook until onions clear, stirring all the while.

Fajita Red Sauce

In a medium sauce pan, combine:

1   28-oz can whole tomatoes, quartered

1   Jalapeno peppers, chopped seeds and all

2   Large onion, chopped in ½" pieces

1   Tbs olive oil

1   Tbs wine vinegar

1   Tsp **Baja Adobo** seasoning

1   Tsp garlic powder

1   Tbs lemon juice

1   Tsp oregano, crushed

1   Tsp sugar

1   Tsp cumin

Cook over medium heat until mixture thickens (about 2 hours.) Serve as a dip and as a condiment with your fajitas.

PASTA DISHES

Lee's Legendary Lasagna

½   Lb lean ground beef
½   Lb ground pork
1   Tbs **Baja Adobo** seasoning

In skillet, mix together ground beef, pork and Baja Adobo. Cook until well browned. Drain well and set aside.

6   Curly lasagna noodles
1   Tsp salt

In large pan bring 3 Quarts water to boil. Add 1 Tsp salt and noodles. Boil for about 10 minutes, stirring occasionally. Drain and rinse under cold water. Dry on paper towel.

½   Tsp **Deep South Soul** seasoning
½   Cup chopped onion
2   Tsp crushed garlic
2   Tbs sugar
1   Tsp fennel seed
⅛   Cup dried parsley
2   14½-oz cans Italian-style stewed tomatoes, chopped
2   8-oz cans tomato sauce

In medium pan mix together onion, garlic, sugar, salt, fennel seed, parsley, tomatoes and tomato paste. Bring to boil. Reduce to low. Simmer for 30 minutes.

1	15-oz ricotta cheese
⅛	Cup dried parsley
½	Tsp black pepper
¼	Tsp garlic powder
2	Cups grated mozzarella cheese

To ricotta add parsley, black pepper and garlic powder; stir well.

In 9" X 9" oven-proof baking dish spread 1 cup tomato sauce, layer with 3 noodles trimmed to fit, using pieces to finish covering sauce.

Spread 1 cup mozzarella, 1 cup meat and 1 more cup tomato sauce.

Add 3 more noodles as before.

Add 1 cup mozzarella cheese.

Put 1 cup meat into ricotta mixture, layer over noodles and top with 1 cup mozzarella.

Bake at 425° for 20 minutes. You can mix the remaining meat into the tomato sauce and save for spaghetti later.

Pasta Positively Perfect

1	Package linguini
1	Stick butter
1	Pint heavy cream
1	Cup white onion, chopped

1   Cup chopped celery
2   Tbs **Tejun** seasoning
3   Cups—cooked crawfish, chicken, shrimp or clams.

Cook linguini according to package instructions. Drain well. Sauté onion and celery in butter until onion clears. Add cream and meats. Garnish with a little paprika.

Serve hot or cold.

KEEP A GOOD THOUGHT

"Keep a good thought"
Say the Sages, "Good things
Will come to you."
But no matter
What the sages say,
They hardly ever do.

I've ever been
The positive one,
Helping those around.
But few have ever stayed to help,
When my ship
Ran aground.

More times than one
I've had to paddle alone
With no one by my side.
I've been so discouraged,
I wanted to run
Away to hide.

Though it's something
I have considered,
I don't think of it constantly.
It's just that there are
So many, who are ever,
Counting on me.

It's not that I am
So important,
Or good at what I do.
It's just that I'm always there,
When lives have been
Knocked askew.

I often wish I could,
Just walk away,
And turn to them a deaf ear.
But something always calls me back,
When I wish I could,
Just disappear.

Sometimes I've even
Wished I could die,
And leave this life of pain.
As I look back it seems,
My life has been,
Mostly in vain.

Not great accomplishments,
No medals,
No award.
A seemingly empty existence,
Could it be,
Death is my only reward?

God, I cannot figure
Out your will,
So I just do the best I can.
Please give me a hint,
A light I can see, all I ask,
Is a hand.

Provide me with,
A guide to the way,
Even a simple suggestion.
Try as I may, every day,
My path is filled
With congestion.

God Please, a miracle if you may,
May it come this very day,
Just one thing, let go my way,
But though I wait out every day,
None comes along.

Let good things come to me,
Good fruit grow on at least one tree,
Make life a little easier for me,
What could I possibly,
Be doing wrong?

Does God really answer prayer?
Does he even really care?
Is God ever really there?
As I lay my Soul bare,
No answer do I hear.

I long to hear God's call,
To pick me up when I fall,
To break down every wall.
To know he's in control of all,
End my fear.

Am I destined to walk along,
Never singing the victor's song,
Everything always going wrong,
Trying hard to be strong,
Though I'm weak?

I search and look about,
For a reason in joy to shout,
Fighting hard against my doubt,
Yet though I am still without,
Him I seek.

For within I will always know,
Though storms about me blow,
Thought life has lost its glow,
Though He seems to work so slow,
Where else can I go?

"PANSY"

We were all set in to have *Pywakit* as our one special kitty when in the midst of filming "Roy and the Rev" in East Texas I visited the Terry Schoof household in Mineola, Texas. I had met them previously when the father, Terry, had volunteered to help on the crew. I had also met their youngest son and considered him to be perfect for a character in the film and had gone to audition him.

When I knocked on their door and was invited in, the very first thing my eyes alighted on was a tiny Calico kitten playing in the doorway of the hall. All else was forgotten as I made my way to it and picked her up. A feistier kitten I have never met and was so tiny she would have fit into a teacup with a little space to spare.

She was the runt of the litter of seven kittens and I fell in love immediately, and after loosening myself from her and completing the audition I had decided two things. I wanted the entire family as part of the film and I wanted that little kitten to come live with us.

My call to Jean began with, "I have found *Pywakit's* baby and will fill you in when I get there."

After explaining the whole experience to Jean, her reply was simply, "Can you bring her and if it doesn't work out can you take her back?" My response was simple. "If I bring her and put her into your hands, you will never let her go."

Jean once had a cat and when another was introduced into the family, the first one took to hiding under the bed and would never come out and she did not want that to happen to Pywakit.

Weeks later, after the new kitten was weaned, I returned to Mineola and brought her back to Dallas. I will never forget bringing her into Jean's bedroom, taking her out of the carrier and handing her to Jean. She was so little she fit into Jean's hand. There was such an instant bonding I am still today hard pressed to describe the experience.

The precious little baby slept all night snuggled up to Jeans tummy and Jean was so afraid she would roll over on her and crush her she slept not at all. Taken to our vet the next day they could not believe she was old enough to be weaned. She weighed only about 14 ounces. A tougher little lady has yet to come around and where the vet said Jean would have to feed her with a syringe, the little girl proved she could eat on her own.

Naming her now became an issue as I thought she should be called "Teacup," for she was so small I thought she could fit in one, but Jean prevailed on two counts. One, she would outgrow that size, and two; she was such a tough little lady she should be called, *"Pansy."*

Jean continued to be concerned that Pywakit would not accept *Pansy*, so I set out to introduce them gradually, telling her that within three days, Pywakit would be giving her a bath. We kept *Pansy* in one of the bathrooms and Pywakit would sit at the door with her nose at the bottom, smelling this newcomer through the crack.

This went on for a day, and then on a Sunday morning, Pywakit was in a glider chair in the sunroom and I went into the bathroom and brought *Pansy* out and put her down in the middle of the floor. Pywakit only looked down at her and never made a move.

Pansy looked around a little while, then made her way over the glider and began looking up. I picked her up and put her into the chair with Pywakit, and miracle of miracles, sure enough Pywakit1 began to give her a bath. Pywakit had found her baby, and finally *Pansy* was the only baby of the household.

They became mother and daughter and had a great time growing up together, with mock battles and chases that delighted us on each occasion. Pansy grew eating dry food and has her feeding station set on the headboard of Jean's bed and when it is empty; she comes in search of Jean and always talks her into going into the bedroom to refill her bowl. She sleeps with Jean and has become her baby and controls Jean completely, sleeping in her inbox on her desk, or taking over Jean's vacated office chair.

Pywakit, on the other hand continues to be my little girl.

PORK DISHES

CREOLE PORK CHOPS

4   ½" thick pork chops
1   Tsp **Tejun** seasoning
1   Tbs olive oil

SAUCE:

¼   Cup catsup
1   Tsp **Baja Adobo** seasoning
2   Tsp wine vinegar
1   Tsp sugar
½   Cup water
½   Tsp celery seed
¼   Tsp ground ginger
1   Tsp flour

Combine all Sauce ingredients and set aside.

Sprinkle pork chops with **Tejun** seasoning and brown lightly in oil. Place chops in baking dish and cover with sauce. Bake at 425° for 25 minutes.

Cuban Pork Roast

5-6 Lb pork shoulder
¼ Cup orange juice (strained so there's no pulp)
¼ Cup lime juice (strained so there's no pulp)
½ Cup New York Lake Country white wine
2 Tbs **Cuban spice**

Mix together orange juice, lime juice, wine and **Cuban Spice**. Using injection needle, inject mixture into roast from all angles.
Place in large plastic bag and let set in refrigerator overnight.
Place in covered roasting pan and bake at 200° for 6 hours.
This is also awesome for baking a ham.

East Texas Pork Chops

6 Center cup pork chops

MARINADE:

¼	Cup ketchup	2	Tbs garlic powder
2	Tbs apple juice	1	Tbs **Baja Adobo** seasoning
2	Tbs olive oil	1	Tbs Worcestershire sauce
1	Tsp cumin	½	Tsp sea salt

Combine marinade ingredients. Place pork chops in re-sealable plastic bag and pour in marinade.

Press out air, seal and rotate bag until marinade is evenly distributed over each pork chop. Refrigerate overnight.

When ready to grill, remove pork chops and discard marinade. Grill over medium heat until done, turning at least once.

POSOLE

1	Lb pork shoulder, cubed
3	Tbs olive oil
1	Medium onion, chopped
2	15½-oz cans chicken broth
1	Tbs **Baja Adobo** seasoning
¼	Tsp oregano
1	Tsp chopped garlic
2	Tbs chili powder
6	4-oz cans green chilies
1	Tbs chopped garlic
2	15½ -oz cans hominy, drained

Brown pork shoulder in olive oil. Add onion, chicken broth, **Baja Adobo**, oregano, garlic and cumin. Cook slowly for 30 minutes.

In blender puree green chilies and garlic. Add to pork along with hominy. Slow boil for 20 minutes.

SALADS

Black Bean Salad

2   15-oz cans black beans
1   Tbs **Baja Adobo** seasoning
1   15¼-oz can whole kernel corn (drained)
2   Roma tomatoes (chopped)
1   Purple onion (chopped)
½   Cup chopped cilantro
1   Tbs chopped garlic
3   Tbs lime juice
2   Tbs olive oil
1   Tbs apple cider vinegar

Drain black beans and corn.

Mix all ingredients together and let stand in refrigerator for 2 hours to let flavors blend together. Take out, stir and serve.

Pork & Bean Salad

To one 53-oz can Van Camp Pork and Beans,
ADD: ¼ cup each of the following, chopped into ¼ inch pieces:

Red bell pepper   Celery
Green bell pepper   Radishes
Onion   Fresh Cilantro

And:

4 Slices crisp fried bacon, chopped
1 Tsp celery salt
1 Anaheim pepper, chopped
½ Cup cheddar cheese, ¼" cubes

Drain all juice from beans in a colander. In a large bowl, mix well all other ingredients. Gently fold in beans being careful not to mush them. Let flavor develop for at least 4 hours in the refrigerator.

VINAIGRETTES

(USING RED WINE VINEGAR OR BALSAMIC VINEGAR)

BASIC

2 Tbs vinegar
4 Tbs olive oil
½ Tsp **Baja Adobo** seasoning
¼ Ground black pepper

HEARTY VINAIGRETTE

2 Tbs vinegar
4 Tbs olive oil
¼ Tsp **Santorini** seasoning

2   Tbs minced onion

½   Tsp Worcestershire sauce

1   Garlic clove, pressed

FOR TOMATOES

2   Tbs vinegar

4   Tbs olive oil

½   Tsp **Deep South Soul** seasoning

¼   Ground black pepper

2   Tbs minced fresh basil

1   Tbs minced fresh parsley

1   Large garlic clove, minced

FOR CUCUMBER SALADS

2   Tbs vinegar

4   Tbs olive oil

½   Tsp **Baja Adobo** seasoning

1   Tbs minced fresh parsley

1   Tsp minced fresh dill weed

Live My Life All Over

What would I do if I had the chance,
To live my life all over?
Why I'd just take off a day,
And I would lie,
On my back
In a field
Of new clover.

I'd watch the clouds make images,
And I'd name them ever one.
And as they each fell apart,
It wouldn't break my heart,
For I'd be
Doing it only
For fun.

I would find a roving river,
And I'd pole it in a boat.
I'd not be in a hurry,
Fluster or flurry,
And not worry
If it tended
To stay afloat.

I'd climb to the top of a mountain,
Not a large one, just a small.
And when I got
To the top,
Why then I'd just stop.
No sense in tiring oneself,
After all.

I'd be sure to plant a tree,
And then I'd always know,
That though I moved on,
When I was grown,
At one time, I started
A young thing
To grow.

I'd take a dusty road, not bother
Where it happened to go.
I'd stop at a plain girl's place,
Get an embrace,
Kiss her gently,
Leave her with her face
All aglow.

I'd take time to listen,
To one who needed a friend.
I'd join them for a walk,
Listen to them talk,
Give them comfort,
Help them see
Around the bend.

I'd visit in a small church,
As just one of the throng.
Leave a gift without asking for fame,
I'd not even tell them my name,
Just join them
In singing a
Worshipful song.

I'd listen to a small child's talk,
Without asking a question.
I'd give no advice,
Nor ever criticize,
I wouldn't even
Make the
Slightest suggestion.

I'd look deep in your eyes,
Take you gently by the hand.
Tell you that our love,
Was gifted from above,
How I never,
Ever felt
So grand.

But all of these I've already done,
Through all of my many years.
I've rowed, and I've climbed,
Even poems, I've rhymed,
Though often my
Eyes glistened
With tears.

But why do I speak of my life,
As if it was now through.
I've yet so much time,
Another mountain, I think I'll climb.
But this time,
I'd like to climb it,
With you.

THREE-DAY DIET

The next pages outline a diet that has worked for me every time I have used it.

As you can imagine, I do love to cook and consequently I also love to eat. My favorite meal is the one that is coming next.

Each of these recipes has been well tested, tasted and enjoyed. Therefore, when I put on a pair of pants I haven't worn in a while, and they feel a little tight, I pull out this tested and trusted diet.

The amazing thing is—It works—*EVERY TIME!* And all the food is good.

It takes some effort to get the food together, but you have to buy groceries anyway, right? So stick with it. I know you will be surprised at the success.

This diet works on the chemical breakdown of fats in the body. Do not vary or substitute any of the above foods. Use salt and pepper sparingly, but no other seasonings.

Use the diet for three days at a time, during which time you should loose from 5 to 8 pounds.

When not dieting, you may eat normal foods, but do not over-do it. Diet only three days each week.

Drink lots of water, ice tea and coffee. Diet cola or other diet drinks are OK.

DAY ONE

BREAKFAST:
- ½ Grapefruit—1 Slice toast
- 2 Tbs peanut butter

LUNCH:
- ½ Cup tuna—1 Slice toast, coffee or tea

DINNER:
- 2 Slices any type meat, (about 3-oz)
- 1 Cup green beans, 1 Cup pickled beets
- 1 Small apple, 1 Cup vanilla ice cream

DAY TWO

BREAKFAST:
- 1 Egg—1 Slice toast—½ Banana

LUNCH:
- 1 Cup cottage cheese
- 5 Wheat crackers

DINNER:
- 2 Beef hot dogs -
- 1 Cup broccoli, raw or steamed
- ½ Cup carrots or ½ Banana
- ½ Cup vanilla ice cream

DAY THREE

BREAKFAST:
5 Whole wheat crackers—1 Small apple

1 Slice cheddar cheese

LUNCH:
1 Hard boiled egg

1 Slice toast (or) 5 Wheat crackers

DINNER:
½ Cup tuna

½ Cup pickled beets

½ Cup cauliflower (raw or steamed)

½ Cup vanilla ice cream

½ Banana or ½ Cantaloupe

SAUCES & RELISHES

CHILI SAUCE—75 YEARS OLD

26 Cups (30 large) ripe tomatoes, chopped
8   Cups (3 large) onions, chopped
3   Cups (2 large) red peppers, chopped
5   Cups (3 large) green bell peppers, chopped
4½ Cups vinegar
2   Cups brown sugar, (firmly packed)
3   Tbs salt

Peel and core tomatoes and place in large stock pot.

In a white cloth, tie 2 Tsp each of:

| Cinnamon | Nutmeg | Cloves |
| Allspice | Ginger | Dry mustard |

Add spices and all other ingredients. Bring to a boil. Lower heat. Simmer until thick (about three hours). Take spice bag out and discard.

Put in scalded jars and seal. Let season three weeks before eating. Use on pork roasts, beans, hamburgers and anything else that sounds good to you.

CHIMICHURRI SAUCE

1   Cup (packed) fresh parsley

½   Cup olive oil

$^1/_3$ Cup red wine vinegar

¼   Cup (packed) fresh cilantro

2   Garlic cloves, peeled

¾   Tsp dried crushed red pepper

½   Tsp ground cumin

½   Tsp **Deep South Soul**

Puree all ingredients in processor. Transfer to bowl. Cover. Let stand at room temperature for a couple hours. Refrigerate.

CHOUK CHUOKA SAUCE

½   Cups chopped onion

½   Cup chopped green bell pepper

½   Cup olive oil

2   Cups medium Picante Salsa

4   Tbs chopped garlic

3   Fresh jalapenos, de-seeded, de-veined, chopped

2   Cups chopped cilantro

1   Anaheim pepper, de-seeded, de-veined, chopped

Place first three items in stew pan and cook until onions clear. Add other four ingredients and cook all until oil is fully combined and sauce thickens (about two hours.)

As a condiment or dip: excellent for sandwiches, pinto beans, all meats and even on baked potatoes.

Honey Mustard

2 Cups salad dressing
1 Cup mustard
¼ Cup honey
1 Tsp lemon juice
1 Tbs wine vinegar
1 Tbs celery salt

Mix all together thoroughly and store in cold place.

Fajita Red Sauce

In a medium sauce pan, combine:

1 28-oz can whole tomatoes, quartered
1 Jalapeno pepper, chopped, seeds and all
2 Large onion, chopped in ½" pieces
1 Tbs olive oil
1 Tbs wine vinegar

1   Tsp **Baja Adobo** seasoning

1   Tsp garlic powder

1   Tbs lemon juice

1   Tsp oregano, crushed

1   Tsp sugar

1   Tsp cumin

Cook over medium heat until mixture thickens (about 2 hours.) Serve as a dip and as a condiment with your fajitas.

PEPPER RELISH

1 Quart cucumbers	½ Cup yellow mustard
1 Quart green tomatoes	1 Quart sugar
1 Quart cabbage	1 Quart vinegar
1 Quart onions	¼ Cup flour
1 Quart green bell peppers	

Chop (coarsely) cucumbers, green tomatoes, cabbage, onions, and green peppers.

Mix all together in large stock pot. Mix mustard, flour and sugar in a bowl.

Add vinegar, mix well and pour into pot with vegetables. Boil for 15 minutes.

Pour into scalded jars and seal while hot.

Taos Relish Story

Once I took my three children skiing at Taos, New Mexico to introduce them to the sport. I had just the year before learned how to ski myself and found it to be exhilarating.

After four or five trips down the bunny slope, Paul and Byron were ready for the top of the mountain and took off, as I stayed with Melody for a few more runs on the bunny slope. We made plans to meet at the restaurant at a particular time and they left.

Although she did not consider herself ready for the top of the mountain, after a couple more runs, I persuaded her to go on to other, higher things.

She did great and when lunch time came we met with the boys as planned.

The air was fresh and crisp and the smell of the hamburgers cooking on an outside grill created an enormous appetite. And there was this Red Pepper Relish condiment. It was awesome.

When I returned to Dallas, and began to look for it, it was not to be found in any grocery store. I began to contact grocery wholesale distributors and finally found one that had it.

To get it I had to purchase two gallon-size cans, and that was a bit more than I wanted, so I put much of it into half-pint jars and gave it to several friends.

After that I decided to make it myself. Here is the recipe. It makes a lot, but your friends will love it when you give them some as a gift.

RED PEPPER RELISH

16 Cups red bell peppers
    chopped in ½" pieces.
1½ Cups sugar

Stir sugar into peppers and let set four hours, then add these ingredients and gently boil for 30 minutes

7   Cups onions chopped in ½" pieces
2   Tbs **Deep South Soul** seasoning
3   Tbs mustard seed
1½ Cups apple cider vinegar
½   Tsp granulated garlic

Put into ½ pint jars and seal. Set in boiling water, covering tops and boil 20 minutes. Remove, tighten tops again and let cool.

TZATZIKI SAUCE

2   Cups plain Yogurt. (Santorini yogurt is best.)

2	Tbs olive oil	4	Tbs finely minced
1	Tbs **Santorini** seasoning		garlic
1	Tbs lemon juice	1	Medium cucumber
½	Tsp **Baja Adobo** seasoning	2	Tbs fresh dill

Place cloth over bowl and drain yogurt (If using pre-stirred yogurt, skip.) for about an hour. Combine yogurt, olive oil, garlic, Santorini seasoning, lemon juice, and **Baja Adobo** in a bowl. Cover and let set for one hour.

Shred cucumber, then squeeze by hand until liquid is gone. Add cucumber and finely chopped dill to yogurt mixture. Mix well.

Serve sliced meat on warm pita bread (not pita pocket) with fresh thin sliced tomatoes, onions and Tzatziki Sauce.

Meant for the Gyro's but great on many things.

MY CHILDREN'S TIMES

As I review, my children's times,
Great joy does fill my Deep South Soul.
For the lives which they are living,
Makes my life much more whole.

But questions still do haunt me,
As I review the past.
Can I say I did my very best,
When I stand before the mast?

Could I have done a better job,
As I sought to guide their mind?
Could I have been more diligent,
Should I have given them more time?

Had I done things differently,
Would their life still be the same?
I wish I had spent more time with them
As down life's road we came.

Did I give my full attention,
As with questions they did approach?
For not having listened more carefully,
Myself I often reproach.

Try as I might, I cannot remember,
Each time they came crying in pain.
I'd make a note of every event,
If I could do it all over again.

As they grew and learned of life,
I tried to let each know,
My love would always be with them,
Wherever they might go.

As years passed and lessons learned
Caused their horizons to expand.
I guardedly, but distantly,
Let them explore each new land.

As they made each new discovery,
I shared in their delight.
When they were sick and feverish,
I held them through the night.

When they were little and I was young,
We ran along together.
As they grew tired, I carried them,
They were light as any feather.

They are now big, and I am old,
Yet still I can hear their laughter.
The memories of our shared times,
I will cherish ever after.

Had I known then, what I know now,
I'd have provided a better start.
But I did the best, with what I knew,
And it was all straight from my heart.

I did not have great possessions,
With which to pave their way.
To my regret, each had to go it alone,
About all I could do was pray.

But I always tried to teach them,
What I have learned from math,
"Keep your mind upon your goal,
But your eyes upon your path."

And when I stand before the Presence,
These words will wake me glad.
"Come right in, you've earned a place,
You were a pretty good dad."

CHRISTMAS RUM CAKE

Before you start, sample the rum and check for quality. Good, isn't it?
Now go ahead. Select a large mixing bowl, measuring cups, etc., and check that rum again for quality. It must be just right. Try it again.

With an electric mixer beat one cup of butter in a large fluffy bowl. Add one tsp sugar and beat again. Meanwhile, make certain that rum is of best quality.

Add two large eggs and two cups dried fruit and beat until very high. If fruit gets suck in beater, pry it out with a screwdriver. Sample rum again, checking for consistency.

Next, stiff in half pint of baking soda and a pinch of rum, one seaspoon of toda and one cupa pipper…or maybe salt. Anyway, don't; don't fret just taste the rim again. Zowee!

Now, one bablespoon brown sugar, or mole asses or whatever sugar is around. Wix melt.

Grease oven and turn on cake pan to 350 degrees. Now pour the whole mess into the oven, and oops, wheredija put the mop? On second thought, and also third and fifth, which reminds me, sample the rum, forget the oven, forget the cake, check the rest of the rum and bo to ged.

WATCHING A THUNDERSTORM FROM ABOVE

Several years ago, I was on an American Airlines flight from San Francisco to Dallas. Our flight path took us just South of Wichita Falls, Texas. It was spring, and in spring every night there is a storm in the vicinity of Wichita Falls. This night was no exception. Since a child, I have always enjoyed the wonder of lightening. That night I had a treat.

I took a blanket, covered my head and shaded the window so I would not miss a single sight. We were well clear of the storm. Below us were the lights of many small towns.

Most of the lightening was confined to the area of the storm, but once or twice a bolt would strike the ground well clear of the clouds.

When I started writing poetry, the picture returned.

From my plane way on high,
With the dark clouds rolling by,
I look out my window,
And I wonder.

About the people living there,
In the houses everywhere,
Are any of the children,
Scared of thunder?

Is there someone home tonight,
To help them through their fright,
To let them know
Someone really cares?

Do little hearts beat fast,
Before they go to sleep at last,
To dream of flying kites,
Or Teddy Bears?
If I could comfort each tiny heart,
I'd let them know they are a part,
Of a plan that reaches
Through the ages.

Tell their parents they're a vital link,
More important than they think,
It's written in man's history on
All the pages.

Children are our great reward,
In a life that's sometimes hard,
As we try to make ends meet,
With much struggle.

So some night when storms abound,
And the rain is blowing around,
Take your children into your arms,
Let them snuggle.

Much too soon they'll be all grown,
And the joys you will have known,
May be all you have that
Will truly last.

Create memories while you may,
For swiftly coming is that day,
When they come to you in fear,
Will have passed

SEAFOOD

CAMARONES BROCHETTES DIABLO

Begin with extra large shrimp (prawns.) After washing and de-veining, increase the depth of the de-veining cut. Lay a sliver of jalapeno into the cut.

In the microwave, pre-cook an equal number of bacon slices until about ¾ cooked.

Wrap each shrimp, using toothpicks to hold the bacon well in place.

Grill until bacon is completely cooked. About 2-3 minutes per side. Serve with garlic butter, recipe follows.

GARLIC BUTTER

To a quarter Lb of butter, add 2 Tbs diced garlic and 1 Tsp garlic salt. Dip the grilled shrimp in the garlic butter. Serve while hot.

CRAB PATTIES

1	4-oz can crab meat	1	Egg
¼	Cup celery, finely chopped	2	Tbs butter
¼	Cup mayonnaise	1	Tbs olive oil
¼	Onion, finely minced	½	Tsp mustard powder
½	Tsp Worcestershire sauce		
1	Tbs **New Zealand** seasoning		
½	Tsp **Baja Adobo** seasoning		
1	Cup bread crumbs		

Combine all ingredients except bread crumbs. Slowly add bread crumbs, mixing as you do, until the mixture holds together well. Form into 1" balls and flatten.

Heat butter and olive oil in frying pan over medium heat and fry patties until golden brown.

Do not fry too many at one time as the heat will diminish. Serve with Aleppo Pepper Spread.

SALMON CERVICHE

1½ lbs. salmon filet.

Cut away black parts of filet and remove any skin. Slice salmon in ½ inch thick slices. Marinate 24-48 hours in covered glass dish in refrigerator.

MARINADE: Combine

2   Limes, juiced
1   Inch grated fresh gingerroot
1   Tsp crushed coriander seeds, lightly roasted;
1   Tsp finely diced jalapeno
½   Tsp **Deep South Soul** seasoning

After salmon has marinated, chop it up and incorporate it into the marinade. Mix well and taste for acidity, salt and spices. Correct if necessary.

TO SERVE:

Put salmon on some nice salad leaves; half of the plate the salmon and half of the plate the Faux Guacamole.

If you want to be very fancy, separate the pink and the green with salmon roe caviar.

Or you can put Cerviche in a small ramequin dish, invert on plate and arrange Faux Guacamole around Cerviche mound.

SCALLOPS

1   Tbs butter
1   Tbs olive oil
1   Tsp **New Zealand Seafood** seasoning
1   Tsp **Deep South Soul** seasoning
1   Cup onion
8   Large Scallops
¼   Cup New York Lake Country White Wine
¼   Cup Orzo
1   Cup Water (boiling)

Put Orzo in water and let water absorb. Melt butter and olive oil with **New Zealand Seafood** seasoning and **Deep South Soul** seasonings and onion.

Sauté scallops until slightly brown. Add wine and stir until sauce turns brown. Add Orzo and serve.

SHRIMP

6   Large shrimp

4   Cups water

4   Chicken bouillon cubes

2   Tbs toasted onion flakes

1   Tbs **New Zealand Seafood** seasoning

½   Cup New York Lake Country white wine.

Place water in pan and add bouillon cubes, onion flakes and **New Zealand Seafood** seasoning. Bring to boil. Add shrimp and wine.

Return to boil. Remove from burner and cover. Let set 5 minutes. Serve either warm or cold.

Great for dipping or using in other recipes.

SHRIMP AND SCALLOPS

6   Large shrimp

6   Large scallops

1   Tbs **Baja Adobo** seasoning

1½ Cups water

2   Chicken bouillon cubes

1   Tbs toasted onion flakes

⅛   Cup olive oil

2   Tbs butter

1½ Cups chopped onion

1   Tbs minced garlic

½   Tsp cumin

1   Tbs lime juice

1   Anaheim pepper, sliced in thin rings

½   Cup finely chopped cilantro

1   Cup Taylor Lake Country White wine

½   Cup toasted pine nuts

Place shrimp and scallops on plate and evenly sprinkle **Baja Adobo** over all. Cover with wrap and let marinate in refrigerator for at least two hours.

When ready to cook, place 1½ cups water in small sauce pan. Add 2 chicken bouillon cubes and 1 Tbs toasted onion flakes. Let simmer for 5 minutes then bring to boil.

Add ¾ cup Orzo pasta and let boil 1 minute. Turn to lowest setting and let pasta absorb liquid.

In large skillet place olive oil, butter, remaining onion, cumin, lime juice and Anaheim pepper. Cook until onions clear. Add scallops and shrimp. Cook until just slightly tan on each side.

Add cilantro, wine and Orzo. Cook and stir until sauce thickens.

Serve to plates and sprinkle with pine nuts.

Tejun Crab Cakes

1   Lb lump crabmeat

1   Tsp Tabasco sauce

½   Cup crumbled Ritz crackers

1½ Tsp **Tejun** seasoning

1   Egg

2   Tbs minced garlic

¼   Cup finely chopped green onions tops and all

1   Tbs **Deep South Soul** seasoning

¼   Cup finely diced red bell peppers

½   Medium Anaheim pepper, diced

3   Tbs honey mustard (pg. 40)

¼   Cup olive oil

½   Cup flour

In shallow bowl, combine everything except olive oil and flour. Gently fold together and form into equal-sized patties.

Drag patties through olive oil on both sides, then into flour. Lay on wax paper to dry.

Pour remainder of olive oil in a large skillet and heat on medium until hot.

Cook the patties for approximately 3 minutes on each side. They should develop a wonderful, golden-brown crust.

SAUCE:

Mix together

½ Cup mayonnaise
¼ Cup chopped spicy bread & butter pickles
1   Tsp **Tejun** seasoning
1   Tbs lemon juice

Chill before serving.

LEE F. DOUGLAS

TELL ME WHAT I WANT TO HEAR

I visited with a dear old friend,
I've known her for many a year.
But when she said
What she did to me,
It almost brought a tear.

I had said something of what I believe,
And she really should have known better.
But her words came out
as sharp as a spear,
I could not understand what beset her.

Then I began to think, and to reason,
And soon came to an understanding.
She'd always believed
What her preacher said,
What the truth might be, notwithstanding.

She had studied the record
Most of her life,
Taught many, both young and old.
But had never had an original thought,
Just repeated what she read or been told.

When I broached a new thought to her,
"Where'd you ever get such an idea?
You been listening to
Those 'radio preachers',
Who suffer from verbal diarrhea?"

Those weren't exactly her words,
But close enough for you to comprehend,
She could not accept
What I had said,
So she sought to condescend.

What was so amazing at the time,
Is what she had told me just before,
"I've got every book
Hershel Hobbs ever wrote,
And I've read each o'er and o'er.

"I never teach a church lesson,
But I read to see what he has said."
What she was saying,
was that in her bliss,
She was parroting, not thinking instead.

She was not taking a passage,
Reading and giving it thought.
So regardless of the truth
Of what HH said,
This to her students she brought.

A thought quickly entered my mind,
"What if Hershel Hobbs was wrong?"
It's not a question
I dared to ask,
I know her retort would've been strong.
I remember what one preacher had said,
As from the pulpit
He shouted,
"Movies are the work of the devil,"
And this she had never doubted.

So in our class she would tell us,
Never go to a "picture show."
Whether or not
She ever went herself,
Is something I'll never know.

But there beside her chair that day,
Was something of which I took note,
There it was,
Handy and well worn,
It was her TV remote.

Herein is a problem that is common today,
And a plague on our whole nation.
Too many believe
Whatever is said,
Though it may be of the truth, a mutation.

They say, "Tell me what I want to hear,
And I'll follow wherever you lead me.
Tickle my ear, lessen my fear,
And I'll swallow
Whatever you feed me."

Is it not time for us think for ourselves,
To learn first hand of life's mystery?
Is it now too late,
Will it ever be our fate,
To never learn from our own history?

THE DANCING LADY

She was really a lonely lady,
Doing many things,
Just so she could
Stay busy.
She loved her dog, her job,
And her children,
And her life was not in
A tizzy.

She took a lot of
Dancing lessons,
The round, the square and
The waltz.
But her life remained
Very empty, and the people
She met there were
All false.

Still she went to
Every lesson,
Worked hard and danced with
Many men.
After she finished all the lessons,
She would start over,
And take them
All again.

No one ever took her
To a real dance,
Dressed up where there was a
Live band.
She just continued to
Take the lessons, then leave,
By herself, with no one to hold
Her hand.

She would be the very
Last one to complain,
Or to admit that she
Was sad.
But somewhere in
Her life long past,
Some man had treated
Her bad.

When one did come,
Who sought to love her,
And was ever thoughtful
And kind.
She retreated to her
Secret hiding place,
Never opening her heart,
Or mind.

He would have loved her
With a love
That would have been
Expeditious.
Searching out exciting
New lands,
But she was just
Too suspicious.

The sadness is,
And she would admit it,
She had hardened her heart
To love.
He was the opposite,
Attentive and warm,
Loving fit him, like a well
Worn glove.

Whatever happened to her you ask,
Did she ever know,
A love that was
Life enhancing?
Did she ever take another chance?
Or did she turn away
Once again to hide,
In dancing?

SIDE DISHES

CUBAN BLACK BEANS

2 Lb black beans
2 Tbs bacon grease
2 Tbs **Cuban** seasoning
1 Large onion cut
   into ½" pieces
1 Tbs **Deep South Soul**
   seasoning

1 Tbs sage
¼ Cup chopped cilantro
2 Tsp **Baja Adobo**
   seasoning
2 Cups medium Picante Salsa

Put beans into a medium stew pot. Add three quarts water with above ingredients. Bring to brisk boil. As water boils away, continue to add boiling water for about two hours.

FAJITA ONIONS

In a small pot, place 4 beef bouillon cubes in 2 cups water, bring to boil and let cubes dissolve.

ADD:

½ Cup white wine
2 Tbs lemon juice
½ Tbs garlic powder
2 Large onions
4 Jalapeno peppers, stems & seeds removed,
   quartered

½ Cup soy sauce
2 Tbs wine vinegar
1 Tbs olive oil

Peel and cut onions into ½ inch pieces. Add to mixture.

Marinate onions for 2 hours at room temperature. (Stir every thirty minutes to make sure all onions have been marinated.

Heat skillet on medium setting and add 2 Tbs butter and ¼ cup marinade. Add onions and peppers and cook until onions clear, stirring all the while.

OH MY ONIONS

12 Medium onions, peeled and chopped
2   4-oz cans chopped green chilies
1   Cup grated cheddar cheese
1   Cup milk
2¼ Tsp **Baja Adobo** seasoning
4   Slices toast, crust removed
1   Egg
1   Tsp celery seed
1   Tsp butter

Boil onions in water with 1 Tbs **Baja Adobo** until just tender. Drain. Line a warm, buttered baking dish with toast. Cover with half of the onions, spread chilies and ½ the cheese.

Beat egg slightly and add milk, 1¼ Tsp **Baja Adobo**, and celery seed. Pour mixture over top, sprinkle rest of cheese and onions on top and bake at 425° for 30 minutes.

Pinto Beans

1	Lb pinto beans
3	Tbs bacon grease
1	Tsp chili powder
1	Medium onion
1	Tsp cumin
2	Tsp **Deep South Soul** seasoning
1	Tsp **Baja Adobo** seasoning
1	Tbs sage

Pick over the beans carefully to remove all rocks, bad beans, bean halves and dirt. Wash several times to remove all the dust.

Put on a pan or teakettle of water and bring to a rapid boil.

Cover the beans with cold water and bring to a rapid boil. Pour off this water and replace with boiling water. Add all the spices, onion and bacon grease.

(Keep a pot of water boiling at all times to add when the water level in the beans goes down.)

Continue to boil beans for about two hours, adding boiling water and cooking down until the soup is as thick as you like it.

If you have it, add some of that left-over ham you have in the freezer about mid-way through the cooking.

Graveyard Workings and Funerals

Being raised by my grandmother had many benefits. She had raised five of her own children before and during the depression and had learned from her mother how to cook some wonderful food.

Also, I was raised in the time when it was the family's duty every year to go to *"Graveyard Working."* This was before the days when someone was paid to keep the country graveyards mowed and clear of brush. So, once a year, people (mostly all kinfolk) would join for a day of work and feasting.

I always loved to go, not so much for the work, but for the food. Tables made from sawhorses and planks were covered with tablecloths and food of all kinds.

My grandmother most often took potato salad, green beans and corn, all of which were grown in our garden. Her potato salad was the best ever—AND—it was NOT LUMPY!

Since I grew up on smooth potato salad, that was the only way I knew it was made, and naturally rebelled at the prospect of eating it with lumps. A little stronger—I just will not eat lumpy potato salad.

I cannot tell how many times I have heard, "Well, you've never eaten *my* potato salad," to which I always reply, "And I never will if it has lumps in it."

As we were raising our children, whenever there was a death in the community, my wife would make potato salad to take, and it was good. But it was only on the rare occasion she ever made it for the three children and me.

One of the family jokes was when I would say on a weekday, "This weekend would sure be a good time for a funeral."

It never worked.

After the children were pretty much grown, their mother actually made potato salad in the middle of the week. When my son came in from school and saw it, he seriously asked his mother, "Who died?"

I have worked on this recipe until I have it down perfect, for me, and hopefully you will enjoy it as well.

I still get a lot of comments from friends about my potato salad. Rarely, if ever, has it not been received with gusto.

POTATO SALAD

4   Large potatoes peeled and cooked until tender.

4   Eggs, boiled and chopped

½   Cup honey mustard (pg. 40)

½   Cup chopped spicy bread and butter pickles

½   Cup chopped onion

1   Tbs celery salt

1   Tsp **Deep South Soul** seasoning

¼   Lb bacon, fried crisp and crumbled

½   Cup finely chopped celery

¼   Cup chopped salad olives

Mash all the potatoes (remember now, no lumps) and let cool for about 30 minutes. Add all other ingredients. Mix well.

Chill before serving.

RICE TIMES THREE

SAUCE:

1   Tbs olive oil
1   Large onion, chopped
1   Tbs chopped garlic
¼   Lb butter
1   Tbs **Baja Adobo** seasoning
½   Lb. medium size shrimp, peeled and de-veined
1   Chicken breast, cut into scallop size pieces
1   Lb sea scallops
1   Cup broccoli, broken into pieces
1   14-oz can bean sprouts, drained
¼   Cup finely chopped fresh cilantro
¼   Cup wine (I like Taylor's New York
      Lake Country White)

Put olive oil, onion, chopped garlic, butter and **Baja Adobo** in large skillet. Heat and stir until butter melts and onions clear.

Add chicken, shrimp and scallops. Cook and stir until chicken is lightly brown, then add broccoli, bean sprouts and cilantro. Add wine. Cook for another ten minutes, stirring constantly. Cover and simmer for 20 minutes.

RICE:

Cook rice according to package instructions, adding 4 chicken bouillon cubes, 1/2 cup chopped onion and 1 Tbs **Tejun** seasoning to water.

When rice is done, serve it to plates covered with chicken, shrimp and scallop sauce.

SWISS ROESTI

6-8 Medium firm potatoes. (I use Yukon Gold.)
1   Good sized onion
1   Tsp cooking oil
2   Tbs butter

Peel and cook whole potatoes in salted water. Do not overcook, they should be slightly hard.

Slice onion and soften in some butter over low heat in a generous Teflon frying pan. Do not allow onions to brown by stirring frequently or covering them with a lid.

The first day, put boiled potatoes in refrigerator and leave onions in your frying pan on stovetop.

Next day grate potatoes on grater using the bigger grates. Add grated potatoes to the onions in the frying pan and mix gently. Add salt and pepper to taste. Add remaining oil and butter. Cook over medium heat, stirring frequently.

When everything is well heated, press gently to make a flat cake. Increase heat and brown bottom of cake. Add butter if needed. When bottom is well browned, invert cake on a big plate and serve.

The inversion is the trickiest part, but with a good Teflon pan you should not have too much difficulty. I prefer to have a crusty top and bottom so I brown both sides.

THE HALF COMPLETED STRUCTURE

I've been down
This stretch of road,
So many times before.
Running down
The interstate
With the pedal to the floor.

Almost late for
An important date,
Everything flying by.
Rarely do I see,
The cars passing me,
But one thing I always spy.

It sets off the road,
And back a ways,
It's been the same for years.
A half completed structure,
And the sight
Nearly brings tears.

Several walls are almost done,
Though worse off
For the weather.
To finish it or not,
It does seem the builders,
Couldn't decide whether.

The roof is not yet started,
Though the shingles
Are lying there.
There are spaces
Made for windows,
But no windows anywhere,

One board has
A lonesome look,
Where the sun has made it bend.
It is such a desolate place,
That whispers
In the wind.

A ladder leans
Against one wall,
The wind had made it move.
And where it rests I see where,
It has worn
A long, deep groove.

Who was the last
To climb it?
Why did they leave it there?
Why is the building
Still undone?
Was there no one to care?

Where did they go?
Why did they stop?
When they had such a good start?
Did they just give up,
Or did it have something to do
With the heart?

Did they ever really
Have a dream,
Or was it just a whim?
Did the cost of the work,
Yet to do,
Hold a prospect much too grim?

Sometimes I wish
I could complete
The work which they did start.
But would all the work,
Yet to do, cause me to
Also lose heart?

I long ago learned a lesson,
That brought me to my senses.
It is impossible for me,
And also for you,
To mend other
Peoples' fences.

We're not the one
Whose task it is,
To discipline the whole of the earth.
As wiser we grow,
We'll come to know, we must first
Prove our own worth.

I look at my life,
The things I have tried,
And the visions which faded by night.
Those dreams of old,
That did not unfold, remembering,
Brings no delight.

How can I,
Without knowing the cost,
Judge anyone's work so aborted.
Till I have walked
Close by their side, and daily
Their efforts escorted.

THE HEALER

She was a healer
Of broken hearts,
This friend I wish
You could have known.
She helped soothe
A lot of my hurts,
But walked
Herself alone.

From whence she came,
I never knew,
She simply came by
One day.
My life was
Dark and dreary,
How she knew,
I cannot say.

She would often
Sit and listen,
As I shared the
Dreams I dreamed.
Never interrupt or
Even comment,
Just giving approval,
It seemed.

There were no
Prying questions,
And her patience
Never ended.
Although we were
Most different,
Our spirits
Completely blended.

When she left
I was much stronger,
I cherish the times
We just sat.
As I think of all
My good times,
I give thanks for
That calico cat.

"Sunny Boy"

Then one day at the office I looked out the sliding glass door that leads to the patio area and there was a 'big' beautiful orange long-haired cat sitting and looking in at me. When I went to the door it didn't move and so I set some food out for it. After it had eaten it scratched together some leaves and curled up for a nap. That evening I left food and water for it and told Jean about it.

"You should have brought it so we could take it to the SPCA," she admonished.

"Well, if it survives the night I'll do it in the morning," I replied not thinking about my words. In the area was a creek and coyotes had been known to come down from the north, having been driven out by the ongoing development taking up their natural habitat.

"Let's go get it," she said, and was not to be denied.

When we got there I walked around for a while, and finally located it on the patio of another office where they had screened it off to feed their own cats. Sure enough, there it was, and when it heard my voice tried to run through the screen. I went over and started to raise the bottom of the screen and he proceeded to shove his nose under and was through in a flash to wrap around my legs as if to say, "I'm so glad to see you, what took you so long?"

We had some friends who had lost their cat and offered it to them, but it was too big for them. Our next option to take him to the SPCA kept getting put off until it was too late.

It turned out that **Sunny Boy** is a Main Coon Cat and is still making himself at home in spite of the fact that *Pywakit* and *Pansy* will have nothing to do with him.

He is both an indoors and outdoors wanderer. He tolerates being inside when it is hot (as if it ever gets hot in Texas) and the place he likes best is the other side of the door.

But, being the 'cat trainer' I am I have trained him to come in the house in the evening by going outside, whistling a special tune and calling his name. Most of my friends do not believe me until they stay around and observe the event.

Then came the day a small black kitten showed up at the front door. Jean had named all of the others and this one soon became *Ebony*.

SOUPS

MANY LONG AGO'S...

When I began to create recipes, I remembered the food and the fun when I was in high school (late 1940's) in Alba, Texas, (population 673). There was an annual spring play day at the Bright Star elementary school, about five miles north on Highway 69.

People in the community would gather, bringing food of every kind. Many brought fresh vegetables and some they had canned from their gardens, all of which were put into large wash pots suspended over fire pits dug for the purpose. The heat was provided from live coals which were taken from fires they built close to the pits.

Beef and chicken was added and the older, more experienced men would watch each pot to assure they were heating just right, as the ladies arranged the other foods and desserts on boards set on sawhorses to serve as tables.

The younger people played baseball and volleyball while the older persons pitched washers and horseshoes and played dominoes.

I knew about the day, called the *Bright Star Stew*. I had never gone because the older boys told me you had to take a lot of food to get to go. My grandmother and I lived alone and had only her Old Age Assistance check to add to the food we grew in our garden, so I didn't think we could spare any.

Between my freshman and sophomore years, I worked for the AAA, surveying peanut fields, and then at several jobs during the following school year. When the day came, I had saved enough money to buy and take several cans of corn.

It was everything I had imagined. The food was plentiful and wonderful. And until the day when I can recreate the whole day—here is the flavor.

BRIGHT STAR STEW

1	Lb bacon
2	Lbs brisket
1	Large onion
2	Tbs **Santorini** seasoning
1	Head cabbage, chopped into 1" pieces
3	46-oz cans V-8 juice
2	14¼-oz cans stewed tomatoes
2	14¼-oz cans French-style green beans, (chopped)
2	15¼-oz cans whole kernel corn
2	15½-oz cans yellow hominy
2	14-oz cans Chop Suey vegetables
2	Tbs **Baja Adobo** seasoning
2	Tbs **Deep South Soul** seasoning
2	Tbs ground sage

Cut into ½" pieces and add:

4	Stalks celery	4	Carrots
1	Large turnip	1	Large potato
3	Medium yellow squash	1	Large green bell pepper

In a skillet, fry the bacon until rather crisp (use in a sandwich). Pour the grease into a 12-Quart stockpot.

Cut the brisket into ½ inch chunks and put into pot. Brown well. Add onion and Santorini seasoning. Simmer and stir regularly until it develops a roux.

Cut up cabbage and add. Bring all to a good boil.

Add 1 can vegetable juice and stewed tomatoes. Add green beans, corn and hominy with liquid. Add Deep South Soul seasoning and Baja Adobo.

Add remaining ingredients.

Let the whole mess slow boil. As the liquid diminishes, add the other can of vegetable juice until all is in the pot.

AVOCADO SOUP

1	Tbs canola oil	½	Cup chopped cilantro
2	Tbs butter	½	Pint whipping cream
4	Tbs crushed garlic	2	Tbs lime juice
1	14½-oz can chicken broth		
1	14½-oz can vegetable broth		
2	Jalapeno chilies, de-deeded, de-veined, chopped		
4	Ripe avocados, peeled and cut into chunks		

In large sauce pan, add oil, butter, garlic, chilies and onion and cook till onions clear.

Add avocados, chicken and vegetable broth and cilantro. Puree with immersion blender.

Stir in cream and lime juice. Simmer ten minutes.

CLAM CHOWDER

Simple and Wonderful

1   10¾-oz can cream of potato soup
2   Cups milk
2   6½-oz cans minced clams (with liquid)
1   10¾-oz can Fiesta Nacho soup
½   Cup finely chopped celery
½   Cup finely chopped onion
1   Tbs **New Mexico Chipotle** seasoning
1   Tbs real butter

Cream potato soup, milk and clams in a sauce pan using a wand-type hand blender.

Add Fiesta Nacho soup and butter. Bring to brisk boil, stirring constantly.

Add all other ingredients. Let simmer on low about 7 minutes to allow flavors to blend.

COLD SPICY SOUP

1 Cup mayonnaise

1 Cup water

⅛ Cup honey mustard (pg. 40)

½ Cup minced celery

¼ Cup minced onions

1 Tbs lemon juice

¼ Tsp garlic

¼ Tsp cayenne pepper

¼ Tsp paprika

Serve cold with crackers. For different taste, add one 14-oz can minced crab meat.

GREEN CHILI SOUP

2 Skinless chicken breasts

2 Quarts water

8 Chicken bouillon cubes

1 Medium onion, chopped in 1" pieces

Combine and boil for 20 minutes, remove chicken and let it cool.

TO LIQUID—ADD:

2	Cups instant potatoes
5	4-oz cans whole green chilies, pureed in blender until smooth
4	Tbs Mexican cornbread mix to thicken.
1	Package frozen whole kernel corn, thawed

Simmer for 30 minutes, then chop chicken into 1" pieces and add. Simmer another 20 minutes.

If it is too thick, thin with a little water—too thin, thicken with cornbread mix.

TEXAS SPICY GRIT SOUP

4	Cups boiling water
1	Cup grits
2	Tsp **Baja Adobo** seasoning
1	Tsp **Deep South Soul** seasoning
1	Cup fresh corn (or 1 15¼-oz can whole corn, drained)
½	Cup white onion, chopped
2	4-oz cans chopped green chilies
1	Cup shredded cheddar cheese
1	Cup Salsa con Queso

Add grits to boiling water with **Baja Adobo** & **Deep South Soul** seasoning and boil about 5 minutes or until soft and creamy.

Add corn. Cook about 3 minutes,

Add onion, green chilies, cheddar cheese & Queso. Cook until well blended.

This can be served as a soup or, if cooked until thick, as a sde dish.

REFRIED BEAN SOUP

2	16-oz cans refried beans
1	Onion, chopped
1	Cup celery, chopped
1	14½-oz can chicken broth
4	Strips bacon
1	Tsp **New Mexico Chipotle** seasoning

Fry bacon until crisp and remove from pan. Put celery and onion in bacon grease. Cook until clear. Add CHICKEN BROTH, crumbled bacon, cumin and beans. Simmer 20 minutes

Serve with grated cheese and tortilla chips.

SEAFOOD GUMBO

Use Bright Star Stew Recipe with these changes:

Omit beef and use three chicken breasts which have been cooked in a Quart of water and 4 chicken bouillon cubes; four 6½-oz. cans minced clams, four 8-oz cans oysters (both with liquids) and 2 Tbs Tajun seasoning instead of the Santorini seasoning.

STRAWBERRY SOUP

1　Quart fresh strawberries, chilled
1　Tsp vanilla
¼　Cup confectionary sugar
1　Quart half & half milk, chilled

Remove stems and leaves. Whirl in blender until smooth. Drain. Return to blender. Blend in vanilla and sugar.

Add milk, stir together and serve with sugar cookies

SOPA DE AZTECA

¼　Cup olive oil
2　Tbs butter
1　Cup chopped onion
1　14 ½-oz can vegetable broth
1　14½-oz can chicken broth
1　10¾-oz can cream of potato soup
2　10¾-oz can nacho cheese soup
1　Poblano pepper
10　Large jalapeno peppers
1　Large Anaheim pepper

2   Serrano peppers

     Take stems off peppers, de-seed, de-vein and chop them.

1   Cup shredded baby carrots

1   Cup shredded celery

1   Tbs **Baja Adobo** seasoning

½   Tsp **New Mexico Chipotle** seasoning

1   Quart heavy whipping cream

Sauté onions in pan with olive oil and butter, stirring frequently until onions clear.

Add vegetable broth, chicken broth and potato soup. Bring to a boil over medium heat, stirring constantly.

Add peppers, carrots, celery, **Baja Adobo** and **New Mexico Chipotle**.

Insert immersion blender and cream everything.

Stir in Fiesta nacho soup.

Reduce heat to simmer for 10-15 minutes, stirring often. Stir in cream. Simmer for 5 minutes or until hot.

Serve with Cheetoes, (Jalapeño Cheetoes if you can find them.) This is also great as a cold soup.

(Does not freeze well. Actually does freeze solid, but milk separates when you thaw it and though taste is same, texture is not)

Taco Soup

1	Lb lean ground beef
1	Large onion, chopped
2	4-oz cans chopped green chilies
2	Tbs bacon drippings
1	15¾ -oz can yellow corn with liquid
1	15½-oz can white hominy with liquid
4	Tbs chopped garlic
1	15-oz can black beans with liquid
1	Pkg. Taco seasoning
2	28-oz cans diced tomatoes

Brown beef. Add onions and cook until onions clear. Add chilies and all vegetables. Simmer for 30-45 minutes on low heat.

And Speaking of Mexican Food

Let's talk **Tortilla Soup**. Quite possibly the best Tortilla Soup *ever!*

There are as many flavors of Tortilla Soup as there are restaurants that serve Mexican food and most of them are good.

I cannot recount the number of people I have served this to, and have guarded the recipe with great dedication, but since you are such a special person, after all you bought this book without reading it...or did you?

You didn't see it at your friends house and took it did you? Well, if you did, make this soup, invite them over and feed them. They'll forgive you of anything.

Ok, now that we got that out of the way —A close friend, W. R. Hendrickson invited me over for dinner one evening.

He made a fat-free Tortilla soup that was good and had a unique taste. He gave me the recipe which was the beginning point for the following creation.

Now this makes a lot of stew, but it freezes real well. When you have a hunger nothing else will satisfy…thaw and enjoy.

TORTILLA SOUP

4	Quarts water
2	Large onions, chopped
10	Chicken bouillon cubes
	(You can substitute chicken broth)
4	Tbs crushed garlic
1	Cup dry cilantro
2	28-oz cans crushed tomatoes
½	Cup crushed oregano
½	Cup chives
5	Boneless chicken breasts
8	Cups Pace Picante sauce
4	Tbs ground cumin
1	Cup fresh cilantro, stems & leaves, chopped
	Grated Monterrey Jack or Mozzarella cheese
	Tortilla chips

Bring water to boil. Add chicken bouillon cubes, onion and chicken breasts. Boil about 30 minutes.

Take chicken out and let cool. To CHICKEN BROTH, add all other ingredients. Cut the chicken into about 1" chunks and add to pot.

Take a hand held blender (the kind that shreds) put into pot, mixing until everything is shredded and there is chicken in every bite.

Simmer about another 30 minutes. Serve with grated Monterrey Jack cheese and tortilla chips.

VEGETABLE STEW

4	Tbs olive oil
1	Large onion
4	Tbs **Santorini** seasoning
1	Head cabbage, cut up
3	46-oz cans V-8 juice
2	15½-oz cans stewed tomatoes
2	14 ½-oz cans French-style green beans, chopped
2	15¼-oz cans whole kernel corn
2	Tbs **Deep South Soul** seasoning
2	15½-oz cans yellow hominy
4	Stalks celery
4	Carrots
1	Large turnip
1	Large potato
3	Medium yellow squash

3   14-oz cans Chop Suey vegetables
1   Large green bell pepper
2   Tbs **Baja Adobo** seasoning

Put olive oil in large stock pot, add onions and **Santorini** seasoning and cook about 5 minutes.

Add cabbage and cook on low until the cabbage wilts. Add one V-8 juice and bring to a good boil.

Add stewed tomatoes, green beans, hominy and corn with liquid.

Cut celery, carrots, turnip and potato into ½ inch pieces and add. Add squash sliced in thin slices, Chinese vegetables and the bell pepper cut into ½ inch pieces.

Add second can of V-8 juice, **Deep South Soul** and **Baja Adobo** seasonings.

THE SHETLAND PONY

It wasn't the pony's fault it ran away with me. It was Lawrence's fault. He had put me on a newly purchased Shetland pony with only a halter and had left the gate open to the lot. Actually I didn't have the halter on, the pony did.

Lawrence Harris was a neighbor of my Grandmother where I lived from the age of 3 until I went into the Navy when I was 17. Grandma was 56 when my mother died and my dad either couldn't, or wouldn't take care of my two brothers and me so Grandma took on the responsibility.

The Harris's lived two houses north on US highway 69 in Alba, Texas, and Lola Mae, Lawrence's wife, undertook to help raise me, as did every other woman her age ('I'm guessing about 35 at the time) in the neighborhood.

Well, to say neighborhood isn't quite the right expression. There were really no neighborhoods in Alba. It was just too small. Well now that I think about it, there was what would kinda pass for neighborhoods. There was the north side of town, where my Grandma's house was, and there were just three streets involved. My Grandma's housed faced the road that ran through town from the south, with Mineola down that way, and to north Emory. There was no east side and there was no west side.

And when I say 'road,' I mean 'road.' Though it was a U.S. highway, up until 1940 it was a slightly red sandy loam dirt road. Course there weren't too many cars then and no trucks to speak of, so a nightly entertainment was to sit on the front porch and count the cars, everyone taking a direction, North or South.

For a long time, probably to the age of 12 or 13, I didn't know of any other towns in the world except for Alba, Mineola, Grand Saline and Emory. I guess I kinda thought the world ended there, except there was Dallas somewhere west where my dad lived.

My Grandma's house faced west and across the road there were the railroad tracks where the MKT railroad made its north-south run one day and then south-north the next day. People in town called it the tri-daily, because it was so unreliable, it would try to make it one day, and if it didn't make it, it would try again the next day.

The other lady who took it upon herself to help my Grandma raise me was Vera Mae Wallace. I kinda liked her best. She wasn't married nor had children, (in those days being married was a pre-requisite to having children,) and fussed over me. She would dress me up and take me to town, carrying me part of the way. I loved the feeling of her arms around me. She did have a boyfriend, but he didn't seem to mind her giving me some of her attention.

During the beginning of WWII her brother, Arvil Lee, cut himself while shaving one morning. Back then the best shave was to be had by using a Blue Diamond double-edged razor and they were terribly sharp. The story is that he didn't have any after shave lotion and wouldn't use the rubbing alcohol his mother brought him for the cut so he got blood poisoning.

We would call it a bacteriological infection today and there would be all sorts of medicines for that, but by the time they called Doc Farrington, there was not much the Doc could do. In three days he died.

Arvil Lee's mother never quite forgave Doc Farrington for not saving her son, so when Mr. Wallace got sick years later, she would not call him and relied on her and my Grandma's home remedies to get him well. Which he did, although it took weeks for him to get over whatever it was he had.

To the west of my Grandma's, across the road and the railroad tracks lived Mrs. Whitworth. Her house faced the dirt road that came off the Hiway at Pearson's station up toward Emory and then came back into the Hiway down at the fork of the Hiway where the Quitman Hiway ended, or started, depending where you were starting.

Across the road and railroad tracks lived Mrs. Whitworth. She was one of my Grandma's friends, and the reason I remember her is that her niece came to live with her later and was my second grade teacher. She was another unmarried lady who took a liking to me.

But what female wouldn't have? I had long golden red curly hair that (until I got my Grandma's scissors and crawled under the medicine cabinet and cut it) hung down to shoulders. It was Vera Lee that took me to French's barber shop to straighten out the mess I had made of my hair.

I was small for my age, and continued to be until I went into the Navy in 1952. When I joined the Navy, I was 5 foot, 2 inches tall and weighed 120 pounds. Eleven weeks later, I was 5 foot 6 inches tall and weighed 160 pounds. I put on four inches in height and forty pounds in weight in eleven weeks. I had never seen so much food in my life. I didn't know people ate three meals a day! I grew up eating a biscuit for breakfast, nothing much more for lunch and sometimes cornbread and buttermilk for dinner. We didn't call them lunch and dinner in those days, they were dinner and supper. I don't know when or where the change came.

Lola Mae was my favorite of all the ladies in my childhood because she mad the best chocolate pie. It had a crust that was flaky, filled with a dark rich chocolate pudding and golden meringue (we called them 'calf slobbers') topping. I didn't get a piece very often, but when I did I savored it for weeks. She and Lawrence lived with her mother, *'Granny England,'* as all the neighbors called her. I think maybe she was a little older that my grandmother, because I remember her dying years before I went into the Navy. I don't remember Mr. England however.

Granny England was a little lady, hardly 5 feet tall and small boned. My Grandma always said she had to keep a full glass of *Devoe Snuff* in her apron pocket to keep the wind from blowing her over.

Grandma used 'Devoe' as a put-down because she dipped W. E.

Garrett snuff. Funny thing about her dipping is that she couldn't stand it that my dad smoked, but you didn't get between her and her snuff if you knew what was good for you.

When Lawrence and Lola Mae had two daughters, about a year apart, Lola Mae's attention to me was limited and soon forgotten. But not by me.

Many years later, I guess I was about 13, and the girls would have been about, oh maybe 8 & 9, I dug a cave across from my Grandma's house in the bank between the road and the railroad. It was not much of a cave, but it was mine, and I wouldn't let them get into it. I told them I had to get the snakes out every time before I could go into it, and they wouldn't go close to it.

Then I told them I had formed a club and only club members could go into the 'cave.' I wouldn't tell them who members were (nor that I was the only one,) but that made them want to go in even more.

Mind you, the 'cave' inside was only about 2 feet in diameter and was, at the most, 4 feet into the clay embankment. But a small opening lent an air of mystery, especially when I closed it with some boards I had salvaged from somewhere. This went on for months, them wanting in, me not letting them in, and their mother telling them they were not even to go near it because "it might fall in on them."

Becoming bored with the game I came upon a new idea. They could become members of the club, and then I would sneak them into the 'cave' when their mother was not looking—but—they would have to go through the ***initiation.***

I cannot for the life of me remember if the idea for the initiation came from something I read, or if it was something I came up with, but it was creative.

My Grandpa had a tool shed behind the garage that used to be closer to the road before my dad came to live with my grandmother and open a tailor shop. When he came home, I helped and we jacked the garage up and rolled it back about 30 feet from the road. I have no idea why.

It was kinda tricky because there was a floor in the tool shed part, but none in the part where the car was suppose to be parked. I say supposed, because I barely remember his car being parked in it more than once.

The land in East Texas is mostly sandy loam and the dirt floor of the garage was like a flour-like powder since it never got wet. It was in this dirt that a great number of "Doodlebugs" (also known as "Ant Lions") lived. They would burrow into the sand and create 'upside-down funnels' where they waited at the bottom for an ant or other small insect to stumble onto their trap. The sides were steep enough and the sand was fine enough that any unfortunate creature that slipped in; in its struggle to crawl out, would only be inexorably drawn to the bottom where they were dragged under sand and sucked dry of all their fluids.

It was great sport to get a straw out of Grandma's broom and if you were careful, you could fool the Doodlebug into thinking an ant was in the trap and when they grabbed the straw we would pull them out like fishing for crawdads.

It was in the tool shed portion where I came up with the idea for dehydrated "coal oil" (kerosene.) In those days (mid-40's,) about the only source for heating homes, other than wood, was kerosene. Some of the more affluent (all who lived on the other side of town) did have butane, but not many that I knew of.

I got some hub caps off some play-wagon wheels, snuck up to the "coal oil barrel" in the back yard and filled one. Then I carefully took it to the tool shed and, checking to make sure my grandma had not seen me, began with the process. I had procured a 2 inch piece of candle from under the counter in the kitchen. Carefully balancing the hubcap on three bricks (even in those early years I made the discovery that a three-legged stool is always stable) I placed the candle under it and lit the candle.

I was sure that if you evaporated the liquid from the "coal oil" there would be a powder that could be shipped cheaply. Fortunately, though the "coal oil" did evaporate eventually, it did not explode or catch fire. Unfortunately there was no powder left to be shipped cheaply. Just as well I guess, because I never got to the point of figuring out with what it could be reconstituted.

To set up the initiation I told them they would have to repeat an oath of silence about their initiation, something I made up about telling nobody about their membership, even to their parents.

When the time was right I had them meet me one at a time in the tool shed. There I had assembled all the elements of the procedure. Four knives from my grandma's cutlery drawer, a chunk of ice from the icebox, and another candle and my grandpa's gasoline fired blow torch.

When I brought them in, the dim light allowed them to see the blow torch with two knives heating in the flame. What they couldn't see under a towel were the other two knives lying on the piece of ice.

I blindfolded them, had them put one foot each on a box and after saying some other words, placed the cold knives against their feet. Thinking I had put the hot blade to their foot their screamed so loud my grandmother heard them and came to check out what was going on.

Hearing her call my name, I quickly hid all the implements of torture and we slipped out a secret door I had cut into the back of the garage. When she returned to the house we slipped out through trap door and into the garden. They went home and I went in to ask my grandmother, "Were you calling me?"

I met the girls later when we were all grown with children of our own, and the second thing each one started talking about was the day of their initiation.

But back to the pony story.

Lawrence was a hard working man, who my grandmother always called "a good provider." In East Texas in those days, that was a high compliment for a working man with a family. He started raising ponies as a way to supplement his income working for "Jim Lambert's Wholesale Grocery and Feed" as a truck driver, delivering to the small country stores scattered throughout the county.

Mr. Lambert had a large (by Alba standards) warehouse that was the end of the line for the TP&L Railroad that started in Grand Saline, just to the Southwest of Alba. It was one of the many so-called Short Line Railroads that served the country before highways became paved and trucks took over.

I knew he got a delivery at least once a week and sometimes two, so one summer I would listen for the whistle and would jump on my bike and ride like crazy to be there when it came in. I would hang around for the unloading, and then Mr. Lambert would pay me a dollar to work for two hours unloading 100 pound sacks of cattle and horse feed, chicken and hog feed and flour. Then there was the salt blocks, cases of canned goods, bolts of cloth and boxes of overalls and shoes. It was hard work and was done by me mostly in the summer when I wasn't in school.

Some times Lawrence would let me ride with him on his deliveries and I got to see things outside the town of Alba and learned to keep track of what was where as we drove around the county. That came in handy later when I went to work for the AAA. (American Agriculture Act.)

Lawrence only had one good eye. He actually did get it shot out with a bee-bee gun when he was a boy. I've never understood how he had obtained a drivers license, unless in those days there was no depth perception test you had to pass. In fact, now that I think about it, I didn't have to take one when I got my drivers license when I was 15.

One day Lawrence told me he was getting in a new Shetland stallion the next Saturday and did I want to break it to ride. He never paid me anything, but there was always the chance that Lola Mae would have something to offer me to eat, and I never passed up a chance like that, no matter what I had to do.

Saturday came and I went up to their house kinda early and waited on the porch. Sure enough, Lola Mae invited me in to eat something and sure enough I went.

When Lawrence brought the pony in, it was a beauty. I went out and he let me lead it out of the trailer and then walked it around to get it limbered up from its ten mile ride in the old trailer.

The pony had not been broken to wear a bridle so he only had a halter on it. That didn't bother me because I was used to using a halter, and after throwing a blanket across its back, Lawrence lifted me up on it. When he turned loose of the halter and I turned the pony's head, he spied the open gate and decided to go home, never mind that he had a passenger.

He went through the open gate, made a hard right turn and headed north towards his home pasture, with me holding its neck to keep from falling off. When he settled into a straight run, I sat up and pulled on the halter to get him to stop, but Lawrence had not tied it right, and rather than tightening across the pony's nose to cause it to stop, it slipped up and into its eyes.

Now I not only am on a horse that is homeward bound at a high run, it is also running blind. Moreover, I can't do a thing to stop it or even turn it. Finally I decided to loosen the halter so it would slide off its eyes. Twice I thought about dropping off, but since I only had on a tee shirt and some cut off pants, and this was after they had paved the road, the thought of hitting that pavement without any protection just didn't appeal to me all that much.

Lawrence had finally got his pickup started and had passed us, but when he stopped to try to flag the pony down, it would just go over to the other side of the road. Seeing that I was left to get him stopped I lay down across the Stallion's neck and grabbed the halter at the nose piece and started pulling it to the right into the ditch. About 200 feet up the road was a creek, and I figured it would be a rough ride across that, but fortunately the pony decided it was time to slow down and I slipped off its back running and dragged it to a stop.

Of course Lawrence had all sorts of advice when he finally got there, but I was so mad I retied the halter, pulled a switch off a bush and jumped on the pony's back, and began to teach it a lesson or two about minding on the way back to its new home.

Later, that same pony stepped on the big toe of my right foot and, well that's another story.

THE LADY IN MY DREAMS

There are many nights when I can't sleep,
And I lie awake and scheme.
Those are the times I think most
Of the Lady in My Dreams.

It's rare now she comes to me,
But the memories are ever so sweet.
When I recall, I almost cry,
For those times have passed too fleet.

Often in the yesterdays,
I'd hear her call my name,
I'd answer then, I remember when,
It was all such a wonderful game.

I have even dreamed of her,
When I was wide awake,
She'd walk right up, and look at me,
And my hand it seemed she'd take.

"Let's talk awhile," it seemed she'd say,
A smile within her voice.
Even though it was long ago, the thought,
Makes my heart rejoice.

Even though she seemed so close,
I never could see her face.
But I'm secure, I believe for sure,
She was a lady of style and grace.

I would do all the talking,
Laughing and gesturing a lot.
She never said a word, but I felt she heard,
Then I'd turn, and she was not.

Now I'm grown, and all involved,
And much too busy it seems.
Though happy I'd be, I no longer see,
The "Lady in My Dreams".

She really did live in days long ago
And experienced sorrows and joy.
And though I cannot remember her,
I was her youngest boy.

There have been so many joys,
With her I would like to have shared.
With someone dear, one who was near,
With one who loved and cared.

How many times when I was young,
I longed to hear her say,
"Don't let your problems get you down,
Together, we'll find a way."

Many times I'd have a bad dream,
And awake with no one there.
To sooth my fears and say, "It's alright"
Let me know someone did care.

But it was not to be, for you see,
Death came and knocked on her door.
That dark day, she went away,
To laugh and love nevermore.

I have absolutely no memory,
Of her smile, her laughter or tears.
I never had a chance to learn of her,
From her kinfolk, her friends or peers.

She is just a haunting vision,
From a picture that rests on my shelf.
Often I've thought how great it would be,
To have asked her some questions myself.

She was in her prime,
Thirty-four when she passed away.
What's sad, is the illness that took her life,
Can be cured so easily today.

So if you have lost the one closest to you,
And have known hurt, deep and so much.
If you can remember the sound of her voice,
Her smile, feel her soft loving touch.

When her memories brighten your day,
Just a thought and your heart beams.
Think of how it might be, if it were that she,
Was just, A *"Lady in your Dreams.*

WINTER BEAR HUNT

My friend, Paul, and I,
Went on a winter bear hunt,
As luck would have it, a storm blew in,
Of which we suffered the brunt.

We couldn't see where we were going,
And very soon lost our way.
I figured we were goners,
And soon to be bear prey.

As we stumbled along our luck changed,
A farmhouse came into view.
We found it just in the nick of time,
And some good luck we were due.

The farmer kindly invited us in,
Made coffee and gave us each a cup.
Then in came the daughter,
Just as I was begging to sup.

She was a ravishing beauty,
And my hand froze in mid air.
But Paul, he never missed a beat,
For the ladies he has quite the flair.

We warmed ourselves until we thawed,
Then asked if we could spend the night.
The farmer said we'd sleep in the barn,
And we both said that was all right.

Now the farmer was a rich man,
With much land, many cattle and sheep.
He talked on and on of his great wealth,
All the time I was half-asleep.

But Paul had eyes for the girl,
And involved her in conversation.
Probably he would return someday,
And was laying his foundation.

Out to the barn we finally went,
With Paul looking over his shoulder.
He was talking about how warm it was,
While I thought it had gotten colder.

The next morning when we got up,
Into breakfast we went.
The daughter had a gleam in her eye,
While Paul, he seemed half spent.

The farmer gave us a lift to our car,
And we thanked him from our heart.
After working with it for a while,
We finally got it to start.

The rest of the trip was uneventful,
As we drove back to the city.
All Paul would say, when not asleep,
Was "Boy, was she ever pretty."

Well, yesterday, about nine months later,
I got a call that shook me.
Listening for what seemed like an eternity,
My wits almost forsook me.

I hung up, recovered somewhat,
Then called my old friend Paul.
"The night we slept in the barn,
Did you stay in your stall?"

"You know, I been meaning to tell you,
What temptation did to me?
When you and the farmer were talking,
The daughter slipped me her key"

"It's alright," I said to him,
"I'm not one to cast blame.
But my curiosity has been aroused,
Did you happen to use my name?"

"Well that's another thing," he replied,
"And I hope you won't get mad.
But, yes, I told her I was you,
You probably think me a cad."

"No," I said, "It's OK with me,
But this you'll want to know.
Her father died last month,
And left her all his dough."

"Wow," said Paul, "I'd better go back,
She'll need someone to aid her."
If I didn't know my friend so well,
He'd have sounded just like a crusader.

"Oh," I said, "There's one more thing,
And this is a twist of fate,
Just last week, she died too,
And left me the whole estate."

SWEETS

ALMOND BISCOTTI

2½ Cups flour
1   Cup sugar
1   Tsp baking soda
3   Eggs
½   Tsp vanilla
1   Cup slightly roasted almonds

Combine flour, sugar and baking soda and mix well.

In separate bowl, combine eggs and vanilla. Beat well.

Add dry ingredients to egg mixture and mix gently until well combined.

Add nuts and spoon batter onto greased baking sheet, forming two 4" x 14" rectangles, side by side, about 4" apart.

Bake at 300° for 45 minutes. Cool 10 minutes.

Slice into ½" pieces. Turn each piece on its side and bake 10 minutes. Turn each biscotti over and bake an additional 10 minutes.

BANANA PUDDING

1   Large vanilla instant pudding mix
3   Cups milk
1   14-oz can sweetened condensed milk
1   12 ounce Cool Whip
4   Bananas
1   Box vanilla wafers

Mix together; pudding, milk and Eagle Brand milk with mixer.
Stir in Cool Whip by hand.
Layer pudding mix, sliced bananas and vanilla wafers

BEST PIE CRUST

1¼ Cup flour
½   Tsp. salt
⅓   Cup butter
3-4 Tbs. cold water

Sift flour & salt together. Cut in butter. Add water with fork until right consistency.

Place on board and roll to desired thickness.

CHERRY PIZZA

2   15-oz cans sour pitted cherries
1   Box yellow cake mix
1   Cup sugar
2   Tbs tapioca pudding
2   Tbs white Karo syrup
1½ Sticks butter
1   Cup chopped pecans
3   Tbs cinnamon

Grease an 11 x 14 cake pan and pour cherries in with juice.

Mix sugar with tapioca and spread over cherries. Add Karo syrup.

Spread cake mix evenly over top. Melt butter, add pecans and cinnamon and spread over cake mix. Bake at 325 for 1 hour.

COOKIE BARS

¼	Cup butter, melted
1	Cup sweetened condensed milk
½	Cup flaked coconut
½	Cup chopped nuts
1	Cup graham cracker crumbs
¾	Cup semi-sweet chocolate chips

Spread butter in 9" square baking dish. Sprinkle in cracker crumbs evenly. Pour condensed milk evenly over crumbs. Top with remaining ingredients in any order.

Bake at 320° for 20 minutes or until evenly brown. Serve warm with ice cream.

English Apple Pudding

¾   Cup butter
1¼ Cups brown sugar
1½ Cups flour
8   Apples, peeled & cored

Melt butter in saucepan. Add brown sugar, stir until smooth, and then mix in flour. Slice apples into baking dish and spread evenly.

Place brown sugar mixture evenly over top and bake at 350° for 30 minutes.

Miracle Cheese Cake

1   3-oz pkg. lemon jell-o
1   Cup boiling water
3   Tbs lemon juice
1   8-oz (or 3, 3-oz packages) cream cheese
1   Cup sugar
1   Tsp vanilla
1   Pint chilled whipping cream, whipped
⅔ Pkg. crushed graham crackers—reserve
    ½ cup for sprinkling on top.
½   Cup butter or margarine, melted.

Dissolve jell-o in boiling water. Add lemon juice. Cool.

Cream together cheese, sugar & vanilla. Add jell-o and mix well.

Fold whipped cream into jell-o mix.

Crush crackers into fine crumbs and add melted butter. Firmly pack the mixture in bottom and sides of a 9"x13"x2" dish or pan. Bake until brown in 350° oven.

Spread filling into crumb crust. Sprinkle remaining crumbs on top.

Chill several hours. Cut into squares and serve. Keeps well in refrigerator or freezer.

PEACH COBBLER

2	Pie crusts
1	Cup hot water
1	Quart sliced fresh peaches or two 15-oz cans, drained
1	Cup sugar
¼	Tsp grated nutmeg
1	Cup brown sugar
1	Tsp cinnamon
1½	Tsp flour
1	Tsp allspice
¼	Cup cold water

Bake pie crusts until golden brown. Break into pieces 1" x 2". Gently stir together peaches and brown sugar and set aside. Mix flour into ¼ cup cold water and stir until smooth.

Heat 1 cup water and add to flour mixture stirring constantly until thick. Add sugar, nutmeg and cinnamon. Blend until smooth. Add to peaches stirring gently until well combined.

Layer peaches and crust pieces and repeat until all is used. Bake at 350 for 30 minutes.

PEACHES & CREAM DESSERT

1   4-oz instant vanilla pudding mix
¼   Cup flour
½   Tsp baking powder
½   Cup milk
1   Egg, beaten
¼   Tsp ground cinnamon
¼   Cup sugar
1   8½-oz can sliced peaches
2   Tbs butter, melted
1   8-oz cream cheese, softened

In a bowl stir together flour, pudding mix and baking powder. Combine egg, milk and melted butter; add dry ingredients. Mix well and spread in buttered Pyrex baking dish.

Drain peaches, reserving $^1/_3$ of the liquid. Chop peaches; spread on top of batter.

Beat together cream cheese, sugar and reserved juice; pour on top of peaches. Sprinkle cinnamon over all and bake for 20 minutes at 350°.

PECAN PIE

1   10" Pie shell
1   Cup sugar
2   Tbs + 1 Tsp melted margarine
4   Eggs
1   Tsp vanilla
1½ Cup corn syrup
1   Cup pecan halves

Spread nuts in pie shell.

Beat eggs with fork until just blended, not frothy. Add cooled melted margarine and vanilla, mixing just enough to blend.
Pour filling over nuts. Reduce 350° pre-heated oven to 325°. Bake 50-60 minutes until inserted knife comes out clean.

SINAMON SURPRISE

1   Can store brand biscuits
¼   Cup melted butter
¾   Cup sugar
½   Cup chopped nuts
1   Tsp cinnamon

Combine cinnamon and sugar. Roll biscuits into 5 inch lengths. Dip in melted butter, then in cinnamon-sugar mixture. Layer in baking dish and sprinkle nuts on top. Bake at 425° for about 12 minutes.

RUM CAKE

1	Pkg yellow cake mix	¼	Cup water
¾	Cup oil	4	Eggs
1	6-oz pkg vanilla instant pudding	1	Cups pecans

Blend all ingredients & beat well. Grease & flour Bundt pan. Sprinkle pecans on bottom of pan. Pour in blended mixture Bake at 325° for 50 to 60 minutes.

TOPPING:

¾	Stick butter	¼	Cup water
1	Cup sugar	¾	Cup Rum

Mix all to make syrup. Remove cake from oven. Make holes in top with fork and pour syrup gently over cake.

Let cook completely in pan, then remove. Sprinkle with powdered sugar if desired.

TOMATO SOUP CAKE

2	Cups sifted flour	1	14½-oz can tomato soup
½	Tsp ground cloves		
½	Tsp baking soda	3	Tsp baking powder
½	Cup shortening	½	Tsp ground cinnamon
1	Cup sugar	1	Cup chopped nuts
2	Eggs		

Stir together flour, baking powder, spices and soda. Set aside.

Cream together shortening and sugar; beat eggs until light and fluffy. Mix in soup.

Add dry ingredients and mix well.

Place in Pyrex baking dish and bake at 425° for 25 minutes.

THE JERUSALEM OAK WEED

My grandmother was
A dear sweet soul,
Who took me to raise,
When she was old,
And knew the remedies
For all my ills.

She had learned them
From her mother,
And like her,
There was no other,
None of which had a thing,
To do with pills.

Folks came to her
From miles about,
Bring children with croup,
Old men with gout,
She had what they needed
On her shelf.

There were too many
Here to mention,
I wish now I'd paid
Better attention,
So today I could make
Them for myself.

She had medicine
For a runny nose,
To reduce the swelling,
When the cow stepped on my toes,
There was even something to
Help with indigestion.

One remedy I will
Always remember,
I had to take it
Most every December,
That's when I usually got
A chest congestion.

Behind our house
Was this great big field,
Each year a harvest
It would yield,
And that's where grew the
Jerusalem Oak weed.

When the time was right,
She knew the day,
She'd call me in,
Stop my play,
And we'd go gather a lot of
Leaves and seed.

Tied in a sack,
And put in a pot,
Covered with water
That was scalding hot,
She kept it boiling,
How long, I never knew.

Then out it came,
Over the pot she'd hang it,
When it cooled down,
Then I wrang it,
The liquid that came out
Was an awful brew.

Back to the boil
This mixture went,
And when the water
Was most all spent,
She stirred in sugar,
For measures she had no need.

When it cooled down,
It was candy,
I tell you now,
The taste was dandy,
And to think it all came from
An old weed.

In a fruit jar
It was hid away,
There to await
That winter day,
When sure enough it would
Come in handy.

Because with chest tight
And body aching,
All my coughing,
My grandma waking,
Out would come the
Jerusalem Oak candy.

I cannot describe
The complete relief,
It was almost beyond belief.
My coughing quit,
My chest relaxed,
Then came sleep.

A sleep that harbored
No bad dreams,
As I remember now it seems,
It was like,
Sleeping on a boat,
Rocked in the deep.

Well, I grew up
And went away,
And forgot about it
Until a later day,
When I started to wonder,
And began my quest.

I asked many,
Read most every book,
There's hardly any
Place I didn't look.
My friends all
Thought me a pest.

"Jerusalem Oak weed?"
They would say,
Look at me funny like,
And turn away,
But I determined to find out,
No matter the cost.

I searched years
With persistence
Almost always
Without assistance,
I finally decided the
Cause was lost.

Having given up
In total frustration,
It was one year
While on vacation,
I visited a friend in Kansas
To see his land.

As we were walking
All around,
I pulled a weed
From the ground.
I knew I had found it,
When I smelled my hand.

"Jerusalem Oak!"
I yelled in delight,
And my friend jumped
in his fright,
"I'd know it from all other
Flora or fauna."

My friend looked at me,
In great disdain,
"In Texas," he said,
"That may well be its name,
But here in Kansas,
We call it marijuana."

WHEN I WAS YOUNG

It wasn't so
very long ago
there wasn't so
much confusion.
And no, it's not
the passing years
that make me
look back in delusion .
It was just that
friends were friends,
and we helped
each other a lot.
There was always
someone to give a lift,
when a friend
got into a spot.
Small town friends
are like that,
though we knew
all about each other.
There is an art to
always being around,
without attempting
to smother.

Life was simpler then,
when I was young
and growing up
was easy.
Sometimes for fun,
we'd take a run,
to the top of a hill
called Breezy.

Up there were
many big trees,
providing much
welcome shade.
Down the other side
and over a bit,
was a beautiful
spring-fed glade.

We'd lie on our backs,
sharing our dreams,
and no one ever
made light.
For our dreams were
about all we had,
and to tell them was
clearly alright.

There was not then
all the selfishness,
so much bitterness,
envy and hate.
Friends listened as
we told of our plans
and said they all
sounded great.

No one ever thought
of ridicule,
or casting a
single doubt.
For we knew the time
was coming soon,
to stop dreaming,
and our lives get about.

Back then youth
was like that,
we weren't in a rush
to grow older.
We gave encouragement
to each other,
sometimes just a hand
on the shoulder.

Then too soon
came the time,
when we went our
separate ways.
But memories still linger
of the fun we had,
and brighten many
of my days.

Where is Jim and
Frank and Paul,
where is Willis
and Dale?
Where is Dessa and
Babbs and Ann,
where is Shirley
and Betty Gail?

The picture I see in
the album I keep
shows me how they
were back then.
Now the girls
are all women,
and the boys are
now all men.

We all grew up,
and journeyed forth,
as with differing lives
we coped.
What of all of their
dreams and plans
did they all come about
as they hoped?

Did they realize the
goals they had,
did some dreams die
on the way?
Are their joints now stiff,
their eyes dim;
has their hair all
turned grey?

Did they ever meet
the one of their dream?
Did they have a life
full of joy?
Or did so many
disappointments come,
their zeal it
did destroy?

Not all of us had
an easy time,
and for some the
costs were high.
Whatever made
the difference,
no one will ever
know why.

I hope they never
stopped dreaming,
for dreaming is
a light to the soul.
Dream all your life,
some will come true,
dream, and you'll
never grow old.

To dream and live on,
not linger and wish,
is the secret of a life
that's complete.
Perhaps they'll share their
dreams come true,
the very next time
we meet.

SUNDRIES

Biscuit Mix

5   Lbs all purpose flour
¾   Cup baking powder
2   Tbs salt
2½ Cups nonfat dry milk
3¾ Cups shortening

Combine all dry ingredients in a large bowl. Sift to assure even distribution of ingredients.

Using a hand-held pastry blender, cut in shortening until mix is the consistency of cornmeal.

Store in tight container in refrigerator.

FOR SIX BISCUITS; FOR 12

1 Cup mix	2 Cups mix
¼-½ Cup water	½ -¾ Cup water

To biscuit mix, gradually add water to mix, stirring with a fork. Use just enough water to make soft non-sticky dough.

Turn onto floured board and knead about 10 times. Roll out to ½" thickness and cut out with floured biscuit cutter.

Bake on baking sheet in a 450° F oven 8 to 10 minutes, or until golden brown.

Bloody Mary Mix

1	46-oz can tomato juice
2	Tsp Worcestershire
1½	Tsp Onion powder
1	Tsp lemon juice
1½	Tsp celery salt
1½	Tsp smooth horseradish
1	Sliver jalapeno pepper
2	4-oz cans whole green chilies
1½	Tsp Pickapeppa sauce

Blend all but tomato juice until smooth. Add juice, blend chill and enjoy. (Delicious even without vodka.)

Chorizo

3	Lbs ground lean pork	2	Tbs cumin
3	Tsp salt	1	Tbs white wine
5	Tbs chili powder	2	Tbs olive oil
2	Tsp finely crushed oregano	2	Tbs water
6	Tbs wine vinegar	2	Tsp paprika
3	Tsp chopped garlic	2	Tsp black pepper
1	Tbs **New Mexico Chipotle** seasoning		

Combine all ingredients except pork. Blend into a paste. Add pork and blend well. All of the pork should be a dark red color. Cover bowl tightly and let set for 12 to 18 hours. (Not in the refrigerator.)

Freeze into patties as you would hamburger meat.

When you are ready to have a great breakfast or different evening meal, put one patty into a skillet and cook until crumbled into pieces. Add beaten eggs and cook to your liking.

A TRIP TO SOUTHERN FRANCE

In 2000 Jean and I took a trip to France to visit with friends in Grasse.

It was a grand time; watching the fireworks competition on the beach at Cannes while drinking *Pastis*, tasting the local wines and beers in Eze, St. Paul De Vence, Menton, and several other towns.

The breads and cheeses made in the area were different and delicious, but there are two places that continue to call me back.

One was the Market at Cannes. Long open sided buildings, with rows of vendors, mostly selling foods they prepared themselves. I could have stayed all day, but would have been so fat (or sick) when the day ended, it would not have been wise.

The olives were my favorite. Green olives, displayed in large wooden vats with combinations of spices and other vegetables, were delicious.

My favorite combined garlic stuffed green olives; onions; red, green and yellow bell peppers; and *"Herbs d' Provence."* I make them today because they are so easy.

Then we met the *"Socca Bread"* lady in Nice. Socca bread resembles thin pancakes but is made from Chickpea flour and cooked on the top of a steel barrel with a wood fire built within.

Chickpea flour can be found in health food and oriental specialty stores.

SOCCA BREAD

2 Cups lukewarm water
2 Tsp **Baja Adobo** seasoning
2¼ Cups Chickpea flour (available in
   oriental grocery stores)
¼ Cup extra-virgin olive oil; plus olive
   oil for frying.

Combine water and salt in a large bowl. Whisking constantly, add Chickpea flour until all is well blended. Stir in olive oil and let stand for 30 minutes.

Put 1 Tbs olive oil in thick-bottom frying pan. Heat until hot.

Pour in batter, forming thin 3" diameter pancakes.

Cook until they release and flip over, frying the bottom side also.

When done, put into paper towel lined bowl and cover until all are done.

Serve with red beans, navy beans or with hummus.

TURKEY DRESSING

½ Stick butter   1   Cup chopped onion

2   Packages jalapeno cornbread (baked 1" thick.)

4   Slices day old white bread   1   Tsp **Baja Adobo**

1   Tsp poultry seasoning   1   Cup chopped celery

1   Tsp sage   1   Cup chicken broth

Preheat oven to 375°. Melt butter and sauté onions and celery.

Crumble cornbread and dry bread together in a large bowl. Toss with poultry seasoning, sage, onion, celery, salt and pepper. Pour broth over all and toss lightly. Adjust seasonings to taste.

Melt Tsp butter in 9" x 9" oven-proof baking dish and pour mixture in. Bake 35 to 40 minutes or until brown.

The Day Mrs. McGowan Got Mad

She really was a sweet lady,
And taught her students well.
So it's probably a great injustice,
That we gave Mrs. McGowan such hell.

That lady knew before I did,
When I was going to try some thing.
When I got caught, out came the paddle,
And boy, would my butt sting.

She was a stern task master,
Just short of being mulish.
She had eyes in the back of her head,
And would put up with nothing foolish.

I had moved on from her class,
And was now over in high school.
And yes, the boys got into a lot of things,
But none of them were ever cruel.

We were just boys and full of life,
Meanness, some would say.
No doubt our crowning achievement,
Happened one bright sunny day.

It was a beautiful spring morning,
We were in a room by ourselves.
Looking around for something to do,
We mixed up all the books on the shelves.

The building was old, way past its prime,
And every board was squeaky.
And everything we attempted to do,
We had to do it sneaky.

Jim was standing by the window,
Using a small mirror to comb his hair.
When he was through, as boys are prone,
Started reflecting the light in the air.

Now across the road and over a ways,
Stood the old elementary school.
In the corner room that was nearest,
Was where Mrs. McGowan did rule.

The light from Jim's mirror was small,
And would not quite reach over to her.
When he tried to shine the light
In her eyes, all he got was a blur.

We were on the top floor,
Of a building that had three stories,
I remember what I had once seen,
When I had helped with the inventories.

It was a mirror of grand proportions,
I recall about two feet square.
I knew how to get into the room,
And I did so with great care.

The mirror was all we could hope for,
It cast a light most supreme.
When directed into Mrs. McGowan's room,
We caught her eyes in its beam.

As she moved about the room
We kept the light full in her face.
The light was so wonderfully strong,
I'm sure it caused her to grimace.

We knew she was on her way over,
When we heard her classroom door slam.
We promptly returned the mirror,
And two of the boys did scram.

When she finally arrived on our floor,
She had the superintendent in tow.
"OK boys, "said he, "You're in big trouble,
Who's got the mirror I want to know."

"I do, "said Jim, "Right here it is,"
Taking it from the pocket of his shirt.
He handed it to the superintendent,
As his eyes he tried to avert.

"Why do you want it?" he asked,
As he calmly took his seat.
"I was using it just a while ago,
I like to keep my hair real neat."

"Were you over by the window?
Did you use it over there?"
"Why yes I did," said Jim,
"When I was combing my hair."

"I'll just keep this mirror," said the Super,
"You can have it when school is out."
When they left we congratulated Jim,
That he was a hero, there was no doubt.

The next morning out came the mirror,
And into her eyes went the light.
When she came storming across the road,
It was a beautiful sight.

Her face was red, her nostrils flared,
In her anger she was aflame.
The two of them hit the top of the stairs,
Looked at me and called my name.

"Alright, R.L., where's the mirror,
And you better tell us in a hurry."
And the way they singled me out,
I immediately began to worry.

Who was the one who had told on me,
Why were they ending our fun?
But I was going to be as cool as Jim,
I wouldn't tell on anyone.

"You have the only one I know about,
And you took it and put it away."
I think that was the first inkling I had,
Why teacher's hair turns gray.

They undertook a thorough search,
And went through every desk.
To watch them act in such frustration,
To us was most picturesque.

Of course they could find nothing,
And soon returned to their places.
We all acted our parts well,
As we sat with innocent faces.

The next day was a glorious one,
And we knew what we had to do,
We kept the light full in her eyes,
As long as she was in view.

This time they found the mirror,
For each time we had put it back.
They carefully took it away with them,
And both their moods were black.

Now we had a real problem,
For we had said all along,
"The light is reflecting off the windows,"
Though they never bought into our song.

So now the next morning,
If no light did shine in her eyes,
Once again she would have caught us,
And we'd be one bunch of sorry guys.

So to keep us out of trouble,
The next day I brought from home,
The only mirror we had that was good,
It was even trimmed out with chrome.

When the light once again struck home,
And what a glorious brightness it shined.
She walked over, pulled down the shades,
To fate she had finally resigned.

I wish she had lived just a bit longer,
So I could have told her this tale.
I'd have told her just how it all happened,
Except I'd have blamed it all upon Dale.

What a Grand Trip It Was

One full year before we actually got to go on our trip to France, we had it all planned. Our tickets had been purchased; hotel and museum reservations made and train tickets procured, when Jean tripped on her thong breaking her shoulder in two places. (I have been often corrected, by Jean, that they are now called flip-flops. These corrections have been accentuated with a punch to my shoulder.)

But I digress from the story. We went to Paris for a week, and then took a trip to Bezier in southern France where Emory and Pat White met us to escort us to their home.

Together with other business associates they long ago purchased a dilapidated ruin in the village of Vieussan. After spending much time, effort and money, they rebuilt it to the rigorous codes of the village. And what a job they did.

On about seven levels on the side of a small mountain, though the exterior was controlled by the codes, they spared no expense in bringing the inside to a most comfortable and delightful design, with the most modern of conveniences.

We spent six days with them enjoying their boundless hospitality. We visited two, sometimes three, other villages each day, touring the enumerable churches (of which there were often multiple in each city) and at least two wineries for tasting.

In the evening we most often returned to their home for an exquisite dinner prepared by Pat who is a creative cook in her own right.

Prior to our trip, I had promised them I would prepare one of my favorite dishes, a creation of my own, Pachugas de Pollo con Quail

Sauce, for one evening meal. On the next to last evening I fulfilled that promise.

However, I failed to take into account the lack of availability of certain ingredients which were essential to the preparation of the dish.

For example, there was not a corner Albertsons to which I could run to get cilantro.

And I had failed to bring another essential ingredient, my own formula for Baja Adobo seasoning.

So I had to improvise, and I was totally disappointed with the outcome.

But, since they had never tasted the original, they were unaware of its deficiencies and thoroughly enjoyed it.

Still, I was apologetic, and promised that, upon their return to the states I would invite them over for the "real thing."

We finished our visit with them, continued our trip, and returned home.

The following is a series of e-mail messages between Pat and me concerning the recipe for "Pachugas de Pollo con Quail Sauce.

From: Lee Douglas
To: pwhite1000@aol.com
Sent: Thu, 21 Jun 2007 8:47 pm
Subject: To the Host & Hostess,
With; The Most & Mostest...

Thank you so much for a visit that was both exhilarating and exhausting.

Never saw so many churches, hills & stairs in such a short time in the whole of my young life. (Young, of course, is in relation to Emory.)

Such a comfortable, quiet and secluded bedroom you provided, interrupted only by the songs of the birds early in the am and late in the pm.

I would caution all who follow to be aware of the five (5), count'um, FIVE, steps out of the bathroom back into the bedroom. As you will recall I miss-counted in the early-morning darkness, (can anyone say 4:00am?) found myself sitting on the cold, stone floor, (which under any other condition and time of day, had I intentionally decided to sit there, would have been refreshing; but at that time and under the circumstances, was quite a shock,) wondering, "Wha' hoppen?"

Miss Pat, your culinary skills were so in evidence I thought I was gaining weight, and would probably have done so had it not been for your wonderful generosity of sharing your time and driving skills negotiating the roads and streets as you proudly showed off the incredible towns and businesses (can anyone say wineries?), of your adopted second homeland.

And Emory, what can I say about your endless translation of the words we would see on roadside signs. And to all the history lessons you incessantly heaped upon my ears, what can I add? Only that, though I continued to thank you, (look under sarcastic in any dictionary,) you continued to generously pass on a portion of the vast amount of information you have acquired since you began your adventure in this foreign land.

But, though you thought I was not paying attention, I must admit I was most impressed with what I must assume is only a partial summation of your acquired knowledge of the region of Mongodoc (sic) and Rosieon (sic).

Though it is impossible to get the whole of your beautiful home into one picture, I have taken the pictures I took on our visit to the top of the mountain behind your house and have put them together into a montage that came out rather well, and will have you a copy upon your return in July.

And speaking of your return, we are still planning on having the two of you for a Sunday morning brunch when I will prepare Chouk-Chouka for a taste bud extravaganza, and will also prepare another evening meal in which you will come to know how "Pachugas de Pollo con Quail Sauce" is supposed to taste.

In addition, though there is no way we can repay you for all your kindness and generous sharing of your time and abode, I have finalized a new formulation of BAJA ADOBO SEASONING and will have one for each of your lovely homes along with the new CUBAN SEASONING I spoke of while there.

Again, your special brand of hospitality made me feel more comfortable than I have ever felt visiting in anyone's home.

Looking forward to your safe return to the states and seeing you again.

Love to each.

Lee

PS: Here is the "P de P con QS" recipe that should overcome the lack of certain ingredients. Enjoy.

- - - - - - - - -

From: pwhite1000@aol.com
To: lee-douglas@mindspring.com
Sent: Fri, 22 Jun 2007 5:06 pm
Subject: Re: To the Host & Hostess,

Lee—Direct to You from Mongodoc-Roseion,

Thanks so much for your "guest journal" response to your trip here. It had us rolling on the floor! I have only a few comments before retiring.

Glad you enjoyed it, in spite of the weather.
Can't wait to see the montage. I have photos for you, too, so don't put your album together yet.

Looking forward to dining with you upon return, but I must say that Emory loved your Pachugas recipe as was, and keeps wanting me to fix it for him. I told him you tore up the recipe, and he wants me to remember. I can't, because I only watched you do part of it. He's afraid it won't be the same Mexican style. Can you help me, Dr. Douglas?

Looking forward also to your Baja Adobo and Cuban spices.

We are so glad you felt comfortable here, and thanks for that compliment.

Will await our reunion in Dallas with anticipation.

Love, Pat and Emory

P.S. The weather has now become what we are used to, and sadly, you never saw. You'll have to do it again.

- - - - - - - - -

From: Lee Douglas
To: Pwhite1000@aol.com
Sent: Mon 25 June 2007 8:05 am
Subject: Request for recipe
Well…there is just absolutely no way in the world I could tell you what all I put into the pot when I was at your home that evening, and there are a few reasons I can actually remember.

1: I was working under the influence of multiple glasses of wine, (the exact number of which is lost in a still remembered alcoholic haze.)

2: Most of the labels on the spices which I found in your cabinet were in languages I could not comprehend (or was it the alcoholic haze.)

3: Maybe both of the above.

4: What I do remember is that there was chicken and bacon and olive oil and some other things like onion, butter and garlic combined with, uuh, let's see, a pinch of that spice that is in the small brown bag with the string tying the top to keep it from spilling out. And let's see, what else…Golly gee…

5: What I do know is this, if you will (and this will require you being in the tropopause of your thespian talents,) follow the script below I guarantee he will love it. (Just don't tell Emory there is a difference.)

SCENE I:

Emory and Pat are enjoying a fine cup of coffee while sitting on their patio which overlooks the valley they so enjoy.

PAT:
(With a lilting laugh slightly under the surface of her voice and her eyes shining as if a star was reflecting in them.)

Guess what, Emory dear, Chef Lee sent me the recipe for the Pachugas de Pollo con Quail Sauce, and since you loved it so I want to fix it for you so I need to go to the grocery store to get a few things.

EMORY:
(Smiling as he remembers fondly that evening in Mongodoc when they first tasted the creation of the visiting chef.)
That's great, what can I do to help other than open the wine and l do my best interpretation of Maurice Chevalier after a tryst with Bridgett Bardot?

PAT:
(Struggling hard to keep the smile on her face and the sparkle in her eye.)
Oh, just rest yourself from your busy schedule of sleeping and napping and I will do everything else.

SCENE II:
(Emory and Pat are seen sitting at their dining table overlooking the patio that overlooks the valley they so enjoy. They both have a plate of Pachugas de Pollo con Quail Sauce prepared by Pat's loving hands in her kitchen where Chef Lee first prepared the dish.)

PAT:
Well, sweetheart, is this as good as what Chef Lee prepared?

EMORY:
Well, darling, you worked hard and went to great trouble to find all the ingredients and spices so I must be perfectly honest with you.
(Pat hangs onto his every work, her spoonful of Orzo suspended half way between her plate and her mouth)

EMORY: (Continuing)
This is not only as good, it is even better. I lift my glass of wine to your wonderful culinary talent.

PAT:
Oh Emory!

EMORY:
Oh Pat. Let's go look at another old catholic church.
FADE TO BLACK

From: pwhite1000@aol.com
To: lee-douglas@mindspring.com
Sent: Tue, 26 Jun 2007 3:06 am
Subject: Re: Recipe
HA HA HA HA HA HA! This is a keeper! P.S. I made it last night and Emory and Marie-Andree swooned, so it turned out a winner. There was not a drop left in the bowl at the end of the meal. Thanks again. Pat

_____

THE JOGGER

This is a story,
You may find,
Hard to believe,
But open your mind,
There's something here
To think about.

The story concerns,
A friend of mine,
Whose career was in,
A steep decline,
And his future was
Very much in doubt.

He had family,
A son and a wife,
They loved each other,
There was no strife,
But his bills, he just
Could not pay.

Then one night,
He had a thought,
It came to him,
While he was distraught,
It made sense, even,
In the light of day.

He'd read of a jogger,
Who had died,
Of a heart attack,
So he tried,
And set out to
Jog himself to death.

The next morning,
While it was still dark,
He set out and ran,
Toward the park,
But in a block,
He was out of breath.

He found a place,
And flopped down,
Stretched himself,
Out on the ground,
It was all he could do,
To simply drop.

Before too long,
He felt stronger,
Then went home,
He couldn't wait longer,
His heart was just not,
Going to stop.

The next morning,
He tried harder,
Ran much longer,
And with more ardor,
He got three blocks
Down the street.

He was sure the attack,
Was soon to ensue,
And so he continued
His death to pursue,
Till he began to feel,
Like an athlete.

His mind cleared,
His sales increased,
He no longer cared,
To be deceased,
He made a decision,
To live again.

To the store,
My friend went.
For a jogging suit,
Much money he spent,
Even new shoes his
Habit to sustain.

The next morning,
Off he jogged,
But in the air
That was befogged,
A truck hit him,
And he died.

There is a moral,
So listen tight,
You could gain
A new insight,
But the lesson
Cannot be denied.

Exercise may
Increase your sales,
Money may even
Come in bales,
You may become
Covered with wealth.

Your heart, could grow stronger,
You could feel better,
Could live longer,
But jogging
Can be hazardous,
To your health.

THE SILVER SHAFT OF HEALING

Had I considered the consequences of my actions before starting the following escapade, even my vivid imagination could not have conceived an outcome so bizarre.

I was the Vice President of a company in Oklahoma City and with the Training Officer out with the flu, I had taken his place, traveling to a smaller town about sixty miles away. I had taken with me, Ray Avery, a salesman who was not doing well and hoped that a few days together would inspire him to do a better job.

We were working an area about ten miles north of the small town where we had rented a motel room. Traveling the Farm to Market roads, I was attempting to indoctrinate Ray in the finer aspects of prospecting, sales openings and closings. I loved driving in the country, and even while I was talking, took notice of most everything.

There were only a few farm houses in the area and many of these were deserted. The former inhabitants evidently had chosen to seek their livelihood in distant cities. Large brick houses at the far end of tree lined drives echoed of the twenties, while others were smaller, their corrugated tin roofs and asbestos siding evidence of a life less well endowed.

We turned off the pavement onto a red gravel road and had traveled only about a quarter mile, when I slammed on the brakes, the car skewing on the gravel road from the sudden stop. Ray let out a yelp of surprise. The reason for the abrupt stop was a house I had seen on the left side of the road. It was typical of the area, but larger than most of the others. On the east side of the roof, two gables let light into an attic room. Although now in a state of disrepair, it once was a fine house and the sounds of laughter and tears of growing families must have once sounded within its walls.

Since a young boy I have always found old houses fascinating. Often curiosity has caused me to stop and walk through some of them. Calendars or other discarded items often revealed when people had last lived there. We walked though the house for about thirty minutes, but found nothing of interest.

However, what had made me stop was what I had seen on the top of the house. Installed on every point and all along the ridge-row, was the most incredible set of lightening rods I had ever seen. There were at least twenty rods, all connected to an aluminum cable five-eighths inch in diameter that led to the ground and was in turn attached to a pipe driven into the ground. The theory was that lightening would hit one rod and the cable would channel the electricity from the house into the ground. Somehow this didn't seem too realistic on a house with a tin roof. Each rod had a plastic ball mounted midway up the vertical shaft. The rod at the front of the house had a distinctive weather-vane wind direction indicator with a crescent moon on the arrow.

After our brief side trip, we went about our business, and then returned to the motel for the night. But I just couldn't get those lightning-rods out of my mind. What I most wished for was to find the salesman that had sold that set of rods so I could hire him. Anyone who could sell the farmer on the idea he needed that many rods on a small house with a tin roof must be the greatest salesman in the world.

I could not stop thinking of the inevitable end of the house, when one day it would fall down and all those rods would be lost forever.

When I could stand the thought no longer, I got out of bed and started to get dressed.

"Where are you going?" Ray asked.

"I'm going to go rescue those lightning-rods," I replied, sounding surer of myself than I was.

"What do you mean?" Ray asked incredulously.

"I mean, I am going to go back to that house, climb up on it somehow, and get those rods."

"You're crazy."

"Are you coming?"

"I wouldn't miss it," Ray replied, already getting dressed.

When we came to the gravel road that turned off to the house from the main road, I drove past it about a hundred yards, made a U-turn and stopped the car. From the trunk I took out a hammer, pliers, a screwdriver and wire cutters.

"Here's the way we're going to do this," I told Ray, trying to sound as if I had done this sort of thing before. "I'm going to walk across this field to the house. You go back into that small town we just came through and then be back here in forty-five minutes. When you come back, stop on the other side of the road and honk the horn twice. Then make a U-turn and blink the lights twice. That way I will know it is you."

As Ray drove away, I took off across the field toward the house. Someone had recently harvested grain, and I continually tripped on the stubble. It had been a long time since I had walked over crop rows in the dark.

A full moon began to show above the grove of trees that grew along a creek bed in the distance. The moonlight made the walking harder for the shadows hid more than the light revealed. I stopped a moment to enjoy the beautiful moon, but returned to the mission when a family of wolves started howling. The sound made me shudder, and chill-bumps chased each other up and down my spine.

At the back of the house, an old discarded wringer washing machine made a handy step up to the flat roof of the porch. Using it, I boosted myself up onto that section. Making my way to the peak of the roof I began by trying to pry up the clamps which held the cable to the rod. Unable to see clearly, this approach proved futile, so I cut the cable on either side of the rod. Working my way up the slanted portion of the roof and across the ridge-row, I gathered the rods. As I carefully slid out onto one gable, from the room beneath me came the sound of something hitting the floor.

The sound was so unexpected I lost my balance, and had it not been for the immediate grip I gained on the cable, would have slid to the ground about twenty feet below. Although the house was empty earlier, perhaps a vagrant came in later and was now about to throw something at me, or do something worse. As I was considering my alternatives for a hasty retreat, the sound of rats squeaking in the room below reduced my heart rate considerably.

On the north side of the house, and the steepest portion of the roof, were three rods which I hated to leave; but time was running out and the possibility of falling was real. Deciding I had stretched my luck far enough, I gathered all the rods together and got off the house. After replacing the washing machine, gathering the tools and the fifteen rods I had "liberated," I walked about half the way up the gravel road from the house to the highway.

I stood for a while, trying to see the non-luminous dial on my watch.

When it occurred to me I had no explanation for what I was doing there if someone came along, I hid the rods and tools in the tall grass across the ditch.

As usual, whenever we begin to consider all the bad possibilities of our actions, there is no shortage of imaginings that come to mind. After two cars came by on the main road without stopping, I began to have some concerns.

"Did Ray have a wreck?" "Did he forget the way to get back?" "Did the car break down?" (least likely, for it was a new Cadillac.) "Did the police pick him up?" (closer to a possibility.)

As my thinking was beginning to change from, "What happened?" to "What do I do now?" a car came from the direction of town, made a U-turn at the designated place and stopped in the right place. No horn was honked and no lights were flashed. New thoughts now began to overcome my usual positive attitude. "Was this a pair of lovers stopping at the first deserted spot they could find?"

"Had a neighbor spotted Ray, called the Sheriff who was now waiting to arrest me?" "Should I just lie down in the ditch, pull weeds over myself and stay the rest of my life?"

None of these seemed right so I approached the car. As I got closer, the light from the full moon shining over the car kept me from seeing the vehicle clearly. It was not until I was within fifteen feet I could see it was my car.

Ray must have been looking elsewhere, because when I opened the passenger side door, he jumped, yelled, and nearly made me soil my pants.

"Where have you been?" I asked, my voice tinged with both anger and relief.

"Why did you do that?" he responded.

"I've been worried you might have had an accident."

"I nearly did just now."

"Let's go get the rods."

"Where are they?"

"Down the road a ways."

"Why are they there?"

"Will you stop asking questions, and drive over yonder?"

Ray drove past the farm house before turning around. "Stop here," I said as I opened the door. I jumped out to pick them up and as I was putting them into the trunk, I realized the hammer was missing.

There was no place it could be other than on top of the house. As I considered whether to go get it, my imagination brought forth the image of my fingerprints being lifted from the handle, and police knocking on my door at midnight to arrest me. There was no choice but to return to the house to retrieve the hammer.

Once I had found the hammer and we were on the road again, I learned why Ray had been so late. After driving around town for a little while, he had pulled into a drive-in cafe for coffee. The local constable and his companion pulled into the space next to him.

The officers smiled and nodded, but drinking his second cup, he became uncomfortable so he left the drive-in, going south out of town. The officers followed him, and only turned around when he got outside the city limits. Ray had taken several country roads to avoid going back through town before he made his way back to the meeting place. By the time he got there he had forgotten the signals. On our way back to the motel we again took the back roads, bypassing the town.

When we returned to the motel, I had a message from the wife of one of my best friends. Chuck Embry had suffered a heart attack and was in the hospital preparing to have open heart surgery in two days. "Lee, will you go see him when you get back in town? He is becoming depressed and you're the only one who can cheer him up."

I left early the next morning to return to the city. Visitations were limited to certain hours, and I was not going to get there at the right time, but was not going to let a little technicality hinder me. I stopped first at my house to pick up my bible and a roll of copper wire. I also took apart one lightning rod and put it and the wire in my briefcase.

With my bible under my arm and looking as pastoral as I could manage, I entered the hospital and asked at the nurse's station which room Mr. Eschler was in. When I got to the proper room, although Chuck saw me, I pretended not to see him and went into the next room.

After talking for a while with a man that must have wondered why I was there, I came out and nonchalantly glanced into Chuck's. I faked a double-take, pretending to see Chuck for the first time.

"Chuck! What in the world are you doing here?" I asked in mock surprise.

"Lee, you idiot. Who were you visiting in there?"

Both started laughing when I admitted I had no idea. By that time I was standing at the foot of Chuck's bed, and had put down my briefcase on the floor. We talked a while and finally Chuck got around to admitting he was worried about his pending surgery.

"Surgery? You're not going to have surgery!" I declared, "That's why I'm here,"

I reached down and opened my briefcase out of Chuck's sight and assembled the lightening rod. I placed the rod in the window, tied one end of the wire to it and took the other end over to the end of the bed and tied it to the big toe of Chuck's left foot.

In my best *"television-preacher"* voice I began. "Chuck, you're not going to have that operation. Even now the ethereal rays of the universe are streaming in through the window, into yon Silver Shaft of Healing, through this wire, into your toe, up through your body and are already beginning to heal your heart in an unheard-of before fashion."

Chuck was holding his stomach in laughter and I had just about finished when a movement to my left caught my attention. I turned to see a young nurse trainee, eyes wide in either fright or wonder, moving cautiously toward the door to the hall.

Almost attacking her I said, "Sister, do you have another occupation you can fall back on. The Silver Shaft of Healing is going to make hospitals obsolete. You believe this man is going to be healed, don't you?" She murmured a soft 'yes sir,' and quickly went out the door. Her answer was to be expected, for no one in their right mind would disagree with one who was obviously deranged.

Chuck was in pain from laughter, and I had lost it and was joining him, when Chuck looked toward the door and muttered a soft "Uh-Oh." I turned to face a 5"4" black nurse who had the no-nonsense look of an Army Drill Sergeant.

"Just what is going on here?" she demanded, and by her voice I knew I had to do something to get her attention in a hurry or it could be trouble.

"Why sister, you are just in time for the most incredible miracle ever witnessed by anyone, anywhere. With yonder Silver Shaft of Healing, this man is already better."

Turning to Chuck I asked, "You do feel better already, don't you brother?"

Chuck managed a nodded yes.

Turning back to the nurse I continued, "You do believe in miracles, don't you sister?"

Reluctant to antagonize a lunatic, and after a glance at her patient to see if he was all right, she managed to reply weakly, "Why yes…yes I do."

"Good, then we will continue, but first, I need to test your faith. Let's see, how shall we test your faith? I know. We'll take up a collection." Seeing a bedpan on a table next to the sink and I picked it up held it out to her. The twinkle in my eyes immediately disarmed her, and her laughter evidenced both hilarity and relief. Chuck's pall was broken.

When I returned the next day, again outside normal visiting hours, I stopped at the nurse's station to be sure I would not be interrupting any medical procedure.

When the nurse assured me I wasn't, I turned to go to Chuck's room and was stopped by the nurse. "Were you here yesterday afternoon?" she nurse asked.

"Yes I was."

"Are you Mr. Douglas?"

"Yes," I replied again, dragging out my answer as I checked for the nearest exit.

"I tell you this honey, the story of what you did yesterday has spread all over this hospital. You can visit anyone, anytime you wish."

Chuck had his surgery the following day. His wife had asked me to be there to go in with her to see him. When Chuck saw us coming down the isle toward is bed in the IC unit, he locked his eyes onto mine and did not look away until I was beside his bed.

His voice was weak, but his message was strong. "Lee, whatever you do, for God's sake, don't make me laugh."

About fifteen years later I spoke at the funeral of a friend's mother in a small town near where the old house was. After the services I decided to see if I could find it again. After driving a while, I found what looked like the gravel road leading up to the house.

The barns and outbuildings seemed familiar, but there was no house. I was about to leave, when a patch of large weeds caught my eye. I got out of the car and walked closer. The weeds hid what was left of the once fine house. All that remained were some sheets of darkened, twisted and rusted corrugated tin roofing and the concrete blocks on which the house once stood. It had burned to the ground many years before.

As I stood in the middle of where the house once stood and looked around at what remained of it, I could not help but wonder what caused the fire. I left sincerely hoping it had not been struck by lightening.

— — — — — — — — — —

PUPPIES

My first experience with puppies was not a happy one. I must have been all of twelve or thirteen when I finally talked (or maybe wheedled) my grandmother into letting me take one from a neighbor's dogs litter of pups.

I would go over to play with the puppies. There was one that was more active than the rest and always ran to greet me when I came over. It was black and as some puppies are, it frisky and fun to play with. It was long about December and I promised I wouldn't ask for anything else for Christmas if she would let me have it. Not that I ever asked her for anything.

My brothers and I were raised by our grandparents and they subsisted on what was called at that time, *"Old Age Pension"* checks, probably about 35 to 45 dollars a month. Christmas was all about what we were going to get from an aunt and uncle who lived in Midland, Texas. They had no children and from as far back as I can remember, each November Aunt Lena would write us to ask what we wanted for Christmas. We spent much time agonizing over the decision with Grandma cautioning that we not ask for too much or we might not get anything. When we finally made our decisions we would each write to tell them what we wanted.

When the box containing our presents arrived Grandma wouldn't let us open them until Christmas morning and we would sit and look at the box and wonder if it was the right size to hold what we had asked for and plan what we were going to do if we really got what we wanted.

One year it was a BB gun for my oldest brother, Ray Jr. (called

Brother by my other brother and me) and a knife with a scabbard for the other brother James (called, appropriately, Little Brother.) I do not for the life of me remember anything I ever received except for one year.

It was 1947 and Ray Jr. had returned from the Navy and was in college and James was in the Navy. I asked for a camera. I do not recall what prompted me to do ask for that, but sure enough, when Christmas came, there was a Kodak Brownie box camera with two rolls of film. There were only twelve pictures that could be taken on a roll and the first roll was soon gone as I took a picture of whatever came into my mind.

Realizing that the first roll went so fast I slowed down. I actually have several pictures today that I took with that camera, the most cherished ones being of my grandma.

All of which however has nothing to do with puppies. My puppy became Blackie, not very original for a black dog, but it was my dog and I could name it what I wanted, and that was Blackie.

When I went back to school in January I would put him in the washhouse where I had made him a bed of old quilt scraps and was careful to leave what food my grandma could spare and water for his thirst.

I do not remember the nights being colder in January than any others, but despite my pleas, my grandmother would not let me keep Blackie in the house at night. My bed was on a screened-in porch, just big enough to hold two beds and called appropriately, *the sleeping porch.* My dad, Ray Jr. and I had built it onto the house the previous summer. It had canvas sides that could be lifted up in the summer and let down in the winter or when it rained, and whatever the temperature was outside was just about what the temperature was on that porch. Naturally I slept under a goodly number of quilts.

One particularly cold night I could not stand listening to Blackie whining outside in the washhouse so I quietly snuck out and got him. I brought him and put him under the covers with me. He was frisky at first but soon settled down beside me and we both went to sleep.

The next morning when I awoke he was still beside me. My plan was when Grandma called me I would pick him up and go open and close the screen door. That way she would think I had just come in from getting him and wouldn't know he had been inside all night.

As I turned over my foot touched something at the foot of the bed that had not been there the night before. Yep. Sure enough Blackie had gone to the bathroom under the covers. I won't detail all the problems cleaning up the mess without my grandma knowing about it, but somehow I managed it.

But great sadness came when one day Blackie got out of the washhouse while I was at school, and though there was not a lot of traffic on the road in front of the house, there was just enough for him to run in front of a car and get run over.

My Friend "Bill"

I graduated from college (North Texas State University it was then) in 1959 and took a teaching job in Monahans, Texas, a town of about ten thousand people at the time. I had gone out under the impression I would be teaching History and Government in high school and either through my misunderstanding or their misrepresentation, I ended up teaching the lowest of three fifth grades in the elementary school located in the low income part of town. I had seventeen Latin students and seven Anglo students, none of whom could add 9 + 7 three times in a row and come out with the same answer.

It was one of the most challenging undertakings of my life. The children had very little encouragement at home and absenteeism was high. I had a period off from ten o'clock to eleven o'clock and with the permission of the principal, I spent the hour going to the homes of the absentees, collecting the children and bringing them back to school. It was not long before the absenteeism went close to zero.

In addition, since their reading skills were low, their interest level was low, so again with the approval of the principal we laid the books aside and took up road maps. I divided them into groups of five (I had 23 students, so my math needed some help too.)

Each group was to plan a trip from Monahans across the country traveling through every state. They learned math by keeping track of how much the trip cost, how many miles they got to a gallon of gas, how long it took to go from one place to the next and how much they spent on food and lodging. They learned geography by reading about the states they traveled through and lost their shyness by reading their reports in class.

All in all it was a total learning experience that went on for six weeks. After which, it was easier for them to move on to other more formal studies.

Nevertheless, it was still frustrating and I longed to be in high school teaching what I enjoyed teaching.

At Christmas time we returned to Denton and I made a visit to my former employer, Dr. Pauline Berry-Mack, head of the Department of Nutrition and Human Studies at Texas Woman's University. I had worked the last year I was in college doing statistical research using already antiquated IBM machines and punched cards that had been created when she was in the same position at a northeast university.

We talked briefly and I mentioned that I would be interested in coming back to work for her the next summer when I planned to return to Denton to begin work on my master's degree.

She responded that I would be welcomed to come back, but what she really needed was someone right then. I said, "Let's talk about right now." We made an agreement for me to come to work in the middle of January, which was mid-year in Monahans.

During the visit a neighbor told me about the Crestview Baptist Church in Denton. It was not in what could be described as one of the best locations. It was on the east side of town in a mostly black community, although no blacks were in the membership. Then just down the road and over the hill was the local city landfill.

Her father had been the last pastor. They were now without one and she wondered if I would be willing to fill in while I was in town. I said yes.

Originally it was a mission of another church in town and had been there about three years. The first pastor had a nervous break down; the second pastor had a heat stroke; and my friend's father had died recently of a heart attack.

We were there two weeks and I preached four sermons to an attendance that actually reached 14 at one service.

Christmas vacation over, we returned to Monahans and I went to see the superintendent. My request was simple. Move me into high school or I would be leaving at mid-semester. He didn't and I did.

Not long after we got back to Monahans I received a message asking if I would consider becoming the pastor of Crestview and an invitation to return for a *message "on call."*

Baptists have a funny way of interviewing for a new pastor. You can be there for two months, preaching twice each Sunday, but you will not be considered for the position of pastor unless you are invited *"on call."*

I returned the following week, conducted the morning services and left for lunch with friends. There were thirteen members in attendance. After I left the building they conducted a formal vote as to whether I would be offered the position. Mind you, this was a position that paid the glorious sum of sixty-five dollars a week.

About three in the afternoon I received a call from the head of the "Pulpit Committee" informing me that they voted to "Call" me as their pastor. Curious, I asked what the vote was. "Seven to Six" was the answer.

I told the caller that I would see him that evening for the service. Interestingly, the same thirteen people were at the service that evening.

"Let me first respond to your invitation. You have voted for me to come here as your pastor, and I thank you, and accept." I then proceeded to bring the message I had prepared.

At the close of the service I added, "Now that I have accepted your invitation and preached one sermon as your pastor, this may go down as the shortest pastorate in history for I now resign as your pastor. I understand that the count at the vote was 7 to 6 and though I have no problem with splitting the church up after being here a while, I really don't care to come into one that is split already."

I left to many smiles, much good will and laughter and returned to Monahans.

On Thursday I received a call from the chairman of the pulpit committee informing me that on Wednesday night they had another vote and the count was 14 to zero and would I please come back and be their preacher.

With the new job and new pastorate, we returned to Denton and set up home. It was to be an interesting time. I went to work getting new IBM machines to handle the processing of all the data Dr. Mack wanted for her graduate students to use in their Masters and Doctoral theses.

At the same time I started visiting all the people who lived in the area of the church and, of course, inviting the people I worked with. The membership grew, though slowly.

The growing attendance caused the old members to feel better about the prospects they would not lose the church. However, the growing attendance brought problems of its own.

The inside of the church was like a gymnasium. Just a rectangular box with two classrooms on either side of the entrance where the young children were taught, while at the front of the church, behind the pulpit, was an eight foot wall made of pieces of plywood behind which were dividers that made for three other teaching areas about 8' x 10'.

Attached to the rear of the church was an unfinished building that was slowly deteriorating. It had a good roof and asbestos siding, but inside was nothing but 2' x 4' studding, no ceiling and bare flooring. After about a year, I mentioned that either we should finish it or tear it off because it was nothing but an eyesore.

One of families I had visited with lived about 200 feet back down the road from town to the church in a house that sat about a hundred feet from the road. Bill and Johnnie Yount and their three children lived there. It was not long before their children started showing up for Sunday School. One day right after Sunday School started, I was outside the front of the church picking up some paper that the wind had blown in when up walks Johnnie and her children.

The children went in, but it was obvious by her dress that Johnnie wasn't going in. She was just bringing her children to church. Occasionally she would come to church, but Bill never attended.

One Sunday morning the children showed up with two other children about their age. They were the children of Dave and Mary (name omitted to protect the guilty), a couple that were friends of Bill and Johnnie's. They would visit with Bill and Johnnie and send their children to Sunday School while they talked.

One Saturday I was passing by and noticed Dave and Mary's car was at Bill and Johnnie's and decided it was time to meet them. I had not been there more than ten minutes when Dave and Mary decided it was time to leave. I did take notice that they did not seem to care for my presence. This noted, each Sunday morning when the children arrived, I would walk down the hill to Bill's and sure enough Dave and Mary would leave.

Bill noticed this also and commented on it. I merely responded by commenting that it would seem that he would have to get some new friends.

Then came the Sunday morning when Bill came to church. I made no comment on his presence until after services were over and he came out. "Guess you were surprised to see me this morning," he commented.

"Well, since you don't have any friends to visit you on Sunday morning any more, you probably get bored sitting at home by yourself. So you're welcome, just don't make a habit of doing it, because we're trying to keep the quality level of the attendance high," I responded with a smile.

He later told me that since I had been such a smart ass he decided he'd come just to spite me. Bill became a trusted friend and associate. It got so if the doors were open for any reason, Bill was there.

When we decided to put the money together to purchase the materials to put in a choir loft, Bill was there.

He was in the lead when we decided to borrow money to finish out the back building.

When it was time to select and ordain deacons to lead the church, Bill was there and one of them.

The church house had a big bell on the front peak of the roof, but no steeple to cover it. When I mentioned that we ought to build a steeple to cover it, Bill was right there as we hung on tight while we built it and painted it.

When it was time to finish out the educational space, Bill was there to lend his ideas and back as we lifted the sheetrock into place and nailed it up.

When we needed someone to lead the singing, Bill was there. He had a good, if untrained voice and I even talked him into singing a solo a time or two.

A better friend I have never had in my life than Bill Yount. I think about him on a regular basis. I have to smile when I think of things we did together that brought such pleasure and the satisfaction of a job done well. I still miss him greatly.

Then came the time when the church had grown to the point where they needed someone else to take them to the next level in their growth and time for me to go to Seminary.

I told Bill what I was going to do and resisted his efforts to talk me out of it. After we had ordained a group of men as deacons, I called a meeting of all members on a Sunday night. I explained what I had in mind to do, and why I believed it was the right thing to do and offered my resignation.

There was silence as no one volunteered to make a motion to accept my resignation.

Then Bill stood up. "Well," he said, drawing out the word. "I never thought my first official act as a deacon would be to make a motion that we fire the preacher, but it looks like that's the way it's going to be, so I make a motion we accept the preacher's resignation."

One of the things I most loved about Bill was that he kept in touch. One of us would call the other about every two weeks as I moved my family to Ft. Worth and enrolled at Southwestern Baptist Seminary.

However, that was not the last of Bill Yount. He was a salesman for a Monroe Pearson Wholesale Grocery Supply in Denton and one of his routes took him through the small community of Colleyville, Texas. One of his customers was a member of the Pleasant Run Baptist Church in Colleyville and in a conversation one day, they told him they were looking for a pastor.

He recommended me, I went out there "on call," and they gave me an invitation to become their pastor.

Bill was a heavy smoker and though I tried every trick in the book, I could never convince him to quit. He died of a heart attack in 1982 and I suffered a great disappointment. Johnnie did not call me to let me know so I could attend his funeral. I have spoken to her only once since that time and that was to tell her how it hurt so I could get past it.

It was at Pleasant Run that *"Preacher"* came into our lives.

From the beginning I had an idea the next few years were going to be interesting and challenging. The church had a history of asking the preacher to leave every two years for the previous 26 years. That's 13 different pastors in that relatively short period of time.

We had two children at that time. Paul was born when I was pastor of Gribble Springs Baptist Church north of Denton 8 miles. He was immediately adopted by all the ladies since he was the first baby born in the congregation in a long time.

Byron was born when we were at Crestview in Denton and was immediately adopted by all the ladies as their own, since he was the first baby born in that congregation, ever.

The church was on Pleasant Run Road, a country road, and two miles north of State Highway 121 (which has now been renumbered Highway 26) surrounded by open fields and a few houses, all sitting on at least one acre lots.

The parsonage was south of the church about 100', so all the congregation could know what was going on at all times. There were a number of large trees scattered around the church property and the scene was as idyllic as a Norman Rockwell painting.

While still in Denton I had the occasion to go bird hunting with one of the new members who, like me, was a native of East Texas. Mark Brown had grown up in Golden, Texas which was only four miles south of Alba. He worked for the Highway department there until he was able to move his family to Denton so his boys could go to college.

Mark and I would reminisce about our times in East Texas and one day I related the story of my grandmother not letting my hair being cut until I was about five years old. Sometime around 1938/39, the government decided to pave the road in front of my grandmother's house. I would spend a lot of time in the front yard watching the work being done.

One day one of the workmen came up the sidewalk to ask my grandfather if I was a boy or girl. Seems the men had a bet on and they wanted to settle it.

When Mark heard this story, he nearly fell out of his chair. "That was me," he said, "I was the one who came up to your grandfather. I one of the men who bet you was a girl."

I finally rooked him in to coming to church by never asking him to come to church. When it was time to start working on the educational space, I started asking him questions as to how to do one job or another (although I knew how to do them). He would come show me how to do whatever it was and it was not long before he decided that maybe coming to church was not such a bad way to spend Sunday morning, and he too became a regular.

One day he asked if I had ever been bird hunting. He had recently gotten a young bird dog puppy and wanted to try it out. I made arrangements with one of the members at Gribble Springs to hunt on his property and Mark and I took the puppy hunting. Its natural instinct was a thing to behold. I had never enjoyed anything so much.

Having told that story around to the men at Pleasant Run, one day one of them told me his son's registered bird dog had just had puppies and if I wanted one he would get me one. I was thrilled and told my sons we were going to get a "registered bird dog" soon.

One morning the puppy showed up and was a beauty. The whole family played with it for a while and then I had to go somewhere to do something that took me most of the day. I was anxious to get back to play with the puppy some more and expected to see it and the boys playing in the fenced in back yard, but neither the puppy nor the boys were in the back yard.

When I went into the house my wife informed me that the puppy was dead. I was in such shock I couldn't do anything but just sit down. It seems that Paul had put the puppy on top of a picnic table in the back yard, climbed up with it and then picked the puppy up and pitched it into the air to see the "bird dog" fly. The fall broke its neck.

When I asked where Paul was she informed me he was in his room and I went directly to his room with the intention of paddling him. He was lying on his bed, head buried in his pillow, crying his heart out.

I melted at his sorrow for the puppy and set on the edge of his bed and began to talk about the puppy being in heaven, and that we could maybe get another and he should not feel so bad about the accident that killed it.

"I'm not crying about that," he said between sobs.

"Oh? What are you crying about?" I asked.

"Momma won't let me watch Television," he replied.

It was at that time all my empathy for his crying evaporated and I gave him a paddling he swears he remembers today. Whether or not he really does or just remembers from the many repeats of the story through the years, he will not admit to.

Soon after, one of the deacons, Kyle Reynolds, decided that with all that area to run and play in, and the loss of the "bird dog", the boys needed a dog. Without announcing his decision he just showed up one day with another puppy, a golden colored Border Collie/German shepherd mix. Moreover, having planned his arrival so the boys would be sure to be there, we had no real opportunity to say no.

The parsonage had a fenced-in back yard that was an ideal place to keep a puppy and the first project was to make it puppy-proof. Paul and Byron joined in the effort and soon we could be sure it would not be able to get out and run off or get into the road.

Preacher took over our hearts immediately. He would be at the door the first thing in the morning, waiting for one of the boys to greet him, then to feed him. He would stay with them when they were outside no matter what they were doing or where they went. There was a large empty field south of the parsonage where they played that had a small creek running through it and along the creek were trees where they let their imaginations run rampant, and when they were there, so was Preacher.

Through the years I told the boys about the path I would walk to school when I was a young boy. It too had a small creek, but no trees. My brothers and the other children that lived on that side of town had walked this path when they went to school, and it was well worn. Across the creek some of them had built a bridge that consisted of two 2" x 12" boards, neither of which would reach all the way across, so they were held up in the middle where they met with two big rocks.

As the time neared for school to start Paul started to wart me about making a path, and put the pressure on me by telling his friends in the neighborhood that I was going to make him a path to walk to school. They would come over to play and they too would ask me about making a path. So I borrowed a tractor with a mower attached. With Paul & Byron sitting on my lap, we mowed a winding path up the hill and over the top and right up to the mowed area of the school yard.

On his first day of school Paul walked up the path to school, accompanied by Preacher. Paul and I had already made a plan and when he got to the top of the hill, he made Preacher lie down and stay. I could tell when Paul went into the school, because Preacher sat and stared until I whistled and called him.

Soon Preacher got Paul's schedule down and would accompany him to the top of the hill, wait till Paul and gone inside then come back. In the afternoon when it was time for Paul to come home, Preacher would go to the top of the hill and lay down. When Paul came out of the school he would set up and wait for Paul to come to him, then they would make their way casually home.

One of the changes I had made at the church was to take a water cooler that was in an inconvenient place and install it under some stairs and build steps so the children could get a drink without assistance from anyone.

One Saturday morning we were sleeping in when I heard the back screen door slam shut. I got up and went into the kitchen to see what had caused it. It was Paul, who had awakened, and being thirsty, was walking across the gravel parking yard to the church to get a drink of water.

There was Preacher, walking right beside him. When Paul went into the church, Preacher lay down and waited. When Paul came out, Preacher stayed with him all the way back and into the yard. When Paul came into the house, Preacher returned to his house and went back to sleep.

On another occasion, after I had taught Paul and his neighborhood friends how to catch crawfish using a stick, a string and a piece of bacon, they were across the road doing their best to get the crawfish out of the hole before they could turn loose.

I was with them, but had to go back into the house to answer the phone and took my eyes off Byron who was in the front yard. I should have known better because there was no fence between the yard and the road, but there was a ditch, then a steep rise up to the road level that I kept mowed just like the yard.

As I was talking on the phone I looked out to see Byron going up the side of the ditch toward the road. At that point, Preacher ran over from where he had been with Paul and bumped Byron so that he fell and rolled back down to the bottom of the ditch. He got up and tried again, but Preacher would not let him get anywhere close to the road.

After about four tries Byron came back toward the house and as I came back out he came crying to me and blurted out, "Daddy, Preacher knocked me down." I picked him up and explained that Preacher was just protecting him, but he didn't really understand.

Not too long after we got Preacher he mated with one of the neighborhood dogs and one of the puppies was almost the spiting image of Preacher, so there was nothing to be done but add him to the family.

When Kyle Reynolds first brought the puppy to us he let us know that he had already named him and we couldn't change the name. When I asked him why he had named it Preacher, he replied, "Well, the first thing I noticed was always making a lot of noise, jumping on his brothers and sisters, pushes them out of the way to be the first to eat, and when he is not barking or eating, he is sleeping, so that reminded me of a preacher."

Well, not to be outdone, when Kyle asked what I had named the new puppy I told him I had named him Deacon because he was always jumping on Preacher, pushed Preacher out of the way when it was feeding time and slept most of the time. Kyle laughed and called it even.

There were to be other puppies that came into our lives. There was Preacher, Deacon, Tom-Tom, Duchess, Popsicle, Brandy and Butch.

Preacher was our first family puppy, and is still first in my heart. Though he has been gone for over forty years, I can still see him in my heart and look to the time when I meet him again at the Rainbow Bridge.

(Oh yeah, when it came up to two years of my tenure at Pleasant Run, sure enough some of the deacons decided they didn't like me and decided to ask me to resign. That, though, is a story for another time.)

"EBONY"

Through the years we have participated in a neighborhood "Catch and Release" sponsored by a local pet store.

We caught and released over eight cats and kittens and then watched as they would return each evening to eat at the food Jean left out at the front and side doors.

One by one they would find other places to eat and we would see them infrequently.

Then along came "Ebony."

He was not as skittery as all of the others and we decided that he must have been dropped off by someone or had become separated from home and could not find his way back. I undertook to see if I could get close to him. The idea was to see if he was friendly enough that we could catch him, have him 'fixed,' get him his shots and then take him to *"Operation Kindness,"* a no-kill shelter in Farmers Branch, Texas, that would be able to find him a home.

I made a great progress and soon he was letting me pick him up and stroke him for a little while before wanting to get down. However, a problem arose we had not anticipated. When we called two of Dallas' animal rescue agencies, they both told us that *"since it is so close to Halloween, we aren't taking any black cats in nor are we allowing any to be adopted out."* I would never have thought it, but in the past there have been so many black cats that have been placed with people who do bad and horrendous things to them at Halloween.

Therefore, now that I had begun to get close to Ebony, he begins to get close to us. The weather is beginning to get cold and the thought of him having to find a warm place to sleep at night begins to work on our minds. Jean moves his feeding bowl and water into the garage and I begin to bring him in for a short time and let him eat.

We got a kitten bed, draped a piece of blue towel over it to hold his warmth, put one of my dirty work tee shirts in it and he would curl up and sleep all night there.

Soon, he had rather sit in my lap than eat when I was out there, so every evening and morning, nothing would do but that I go out and spend time with him. Sitting on a cushion I would stretch out my legs and he would crawl on them and then stretch out between them and look up at me as I ran my hands down the length of his back. I think he would have stayed there all day or night if I could have stayed. They were long, loving sessions and I liked them as much as he.

Then we noticed something was not quite right. Where he had run briskly across the street and up the sidewalk when we were feeding him at the front porch, he was having trouble with his back legs. He would be walking along and his back legs would splay out to one side or another and he would sit for a little while as if trying to figure out what had happened.

As it seemed he was having more and more problems, we took him into Jean's dressing room that has a futon bed and made him a bed in the chair. He was happy to be there and rarely came out, except to eat. After about a week he had a bowel movement and part of his bowel pushed out and would not return so we took him to our vet.

She could give us no reason for this, but noticed the iris of his left eyes was not opening as large as his right eye. She thought he might have had a stroke which could be the reason for his legs not working right and also the difference in his eyes. She gave us medicine for his bowel problem and we returned home to begin caring for him.

Sometimes he would get up and come down the hall, falling several times before he got into the kitchen where we were and then sit against the wall and watch us and the other cats. Strangely enough, though our other three cats are very territorial and jealous of our attention, they never attacked Ebony or even fussed at him when they came close to him. I believe that somehow they knew he was not well, and did not cause him any more stress.

During this time he would appear to be feeling better and Jean got a strip of cloth off of a worn out pillow case and he would play with it for a little while, but would soon tire. Jean got him a collar with a bell on it and we put it on him.

The sad conclusion came about ten days later when we had to take him to have him put to sleep. By this time he had become listless, drank water only rarely and ate less. For the last four nights of his life I slept on the futon bed and let him sleep nestled against my stomach. Each night he would look up at me with his soft eyes until he would succumb to sleep.

When we took him in the doctor explained the process and gave us the option of waiting outside, but we would have none of that. As he succumbed to sleep I continued to call his name and then as she administered the last injection I whispered in his ear, "Tell Miss Geraldine we still think of her."

He took one last deep breath and went to sleep.

We took him home with many tears streaming down our faces. He had needed us, and he found us, and the thought that rather than having to die alone, under a building or a bush, but in loving arms, brought some comfort to our hearts.

I built a box out of some cedar I had in the shop to fit a plastic tub from the attic; cut the blue towel to fit and padded the box; left the only collar he had ever worn on his neck, and Jean put his only toy in with him, the string he would play with sometimes when he felt like it.

Outside the futon room which we were calling his bedroom, I dug a hole about two feet deep. I put six inches of sand in the bottom, placed the wooden box in it with the plastic tub turned upside down over it, poured sand in to cover it and them put dirt and grass back over all.

In such a short time a little abandoned guy had captured our hearts in a way I have never experienced before, and brought an experience I hope never to have to repeat.

Yet in all the sorrow and heartache the thought that we were there when we were needed helps somewhat.

Oh yes, when I whispered in Ebony's, *"Tell Miss Geraldine we still think of her,"* I was referring to another cat in our lives.

> *"It's on the mountaintop,*
> *we discover who God is.*
> *But it's in the Valleys,*
> *we discover who we are."*

Lee Douglas

"ROY 'N' THE REV"

INTRODUCING A FILM FOR YOUR WHOLE FAMILY

A few years ago I undertook a journey into the making of a movie. Having created Video Training Tapes for two major international companies, all of which incorporated humor, I thought, "Why not?"

Well, one reason is there are so few family films coming into theaters, is the lack of distributors who are interested. If it is not a slasher, trasher, or basher; they just don't want to talk with you.

So now is your chance to have the Collectors Edition of *"Roy and the Rev,"* a romantic-comedy that will thrill and delight the whole family.

The Story

Rolle Blake is a young white man in his early thirties. A known con-man in the Dallas area, he decides to enter the illegal drug-making business. His plans are cut short when he is apprehended with drug-making equipment in his possession. While being questioned by the police, a woman identified only as "Ms. E" puts up his bail. In a meeting between the two, "Ms. E" tells Rolle she will keep him out on bail if he will do a job for her.

"Ms. E" has arranged for Rolle to pose as the "preacher" at a small church in East Texas. The only thing Rolle has to do is discourage people from attending. Due to deed restrictions set up by her father when he donated the land for the church, if there are not fifty people in attendance on a Sunday three months away, the property reverts to her ownership. She plans to tear down the church and adjacent houses and erect expensive condos.

Sensing an opportunity to get out of town, Rolle agrees. After a meeting with the few members still attending and convincing them he is legitimate, he sets up new drug making equipment in the mobile home at the back of the property and is set to try again.

When a young girl in the town dies from an overdose of drugs, her parents ask Rolle to hold the funeral service. Although he tries to get out of it, they insist and Rolle gets a close-up and personal look at the end results of his newly chosen profession. This experience changes him forever.

When teams are chosen for the youth baseball league in the area, there are several boys who are not chosen to play due to their lack of skills. One of the men in the community, Wilburn Barnett, volunteers to work with them and recruits Rolle to help him. Soon after they start practicing, Wilburn has a heart attack and Rolle is left to coach the team by himself.

The coach's wife, Wanda Barnett, decides she is going to coach the team but when Rolle and the boys decline to continue, she becomes Rolle's nemesis.

Rolle cons Roy Blainsley, a black man in his mid 40's who once played semi-professional baseball, into helping him. Roy soon takes over the practices and introduces some rather unorthodox methods of increasing the boys' skills. They begin to win their ball games, soon by some impressive margins.

Because of their winning ways, the boys get cocky and Roy arranges for an exhibition game with a girls' baseball team. The boys are more interested in watching the girls than playing ball and lose decisively.

One of the detectives who arrested Rolle in Dallas accidentally sees him while traveling through town. He approaches Wanda to help set a trap for Rolle, and she eagerly agrees.

Rolle develops an attraction to one of the player's mother, although she has been ostracized by the community for years because of a decision she made in the past that affected the entire town.

In spite of his lack of effort, the members continue to attend; and new people even start coming. To add to the humor of the story one of the older ladies in the church worries that one of the new people will get her seat; and one of the local hairdressers, develops an infatuation with him and pursues him with comic results.

The season ends in a tie and the boys have to play, for the second time, a team whose pitcher none of the teams in the league have been able to hit. The suspense of the playoff game will prevent anyone from leaving their seat till the last scene.

And well they shouldn't, for there is a twist at the end that will surprise everyone.

You can learn more information by visiting our website at www.royandtherev.com.

SPICES

SPICES

The Wikipedia website offers what they call an, "incomplete list" of the spices of the world that numbers over 190 names.

Since 1980 I have worked to create various combinations of about 60 of these into flavors reminiscent of the areas they are named for.

You may not be familiar with some of the spices mentioned in many of the recipes but you can learn about them by visiting our website at:

www.downhomespices.com.

There you will find information concerning the special seasonings I have developed through the years and are now making available to everyone.

In order to provide a more-perfect union of flavors and tastes, I have dedicated my efforts to the formulation of all-natural seasonings into combinations that will come to full flavor in your favorite recipes.

You can be assured that the seasonings are the freshest that can be obtained, contain no chemicals and are mixed under controlled conditions in sanitary facilities.

SEASONING DESCRIPTIONS

After a period of successful sales of Dr. Douglas Wonder Bakers on a national shopping channel, I was asked to develop more products for presentation. Seasonings were a natural selection since I was beginning to grow bored with the ones that were available at the time.

The first two were based on spices I had used that were on store shelves, but with which I was not completely satisfied.

TEJUN

Sometime during the mid-80's Cajun and Creole foods began to make their way out of the bayous of southern Louisiana and onto the menus of restaurants across the country. They rapidly became popular with many.

When I began to experiment with flavors, I bought many different brands of both Cajun and Creole seasonings; but none was quite right, so I determined to create my own version.

An unusual combination of salt, paprika, black pepper, garlic and 6 other spices, *TEJUN* truly delivers that *"South Louisiana Flavor,"* and livens up every recipe, evoking that *"cooked right on the bayou"* flavor.

Excellent for grilling or baking fish (my personal favorite is on Orange Roughy). *TEJUN* adds a distinctive flavor to hamburgers; is great for enhancing the flavor of cottage cheese (another 'personal favorite' use) and adds extra flavor to all bean dishes.

SANTORINI

In man's search for exotic flavors, Greece was at the center of the land-based traders, and at the crossroads of the sea-based spice traders of ancient times.

Today, *SANTORINI* is a destination island for many who long for ocean vistas of the Mediterranean that stretch the imagination, and is famous for sunshine and savory foods and builds memories which seldom fade.

This unique combination of salt, red & green peppers, oregano, black pepper, onion and 7 other spices all meld together to increase your appreciation of fine foods. *SANTORINI* brings that *"Old World"* taste to every dish you prepare and adds a Greek flavor to omelets stews sauces and salads and brings out the natural flavors of all meats and Seafood.

TEXAS

In the 1980's, with the TV show *'Dallas'* having such international popularity, I thought there should be a spice that imparted a special Texas flavor. Since there was none to be found I decided to create one! *TEXAS* soon became a favorite with all who tried it.

TEXAS is a distinctive blend of salt, paprika, black pepper, garlic and 5 other spices that will impart that *"Outdoor Taste"* that is so popular today. It brings to mind food cooked over an open fire.

It is great on beef, chicken and pork; increases the enjoyment that comes from game and fish and spiffs up salads, soups and sauces.

A great use is to combine a tablespoon of *TEXAS* with a 1/2 cup of virgin olive oil, a splash of balsamic vinegar and let sit for an hour. Spread over the salad of your choice.

- - - - - - -

Continuing to look for variations on flavors, I stumbled onto a Mexican spice that was good, but just not quite right. Therefore, I began to experiment and soon settled on the following:

BAJA ADOBO

There is just a special taste to food cooked on the beach. Whether it is the salt in the air (and maybe the sand that inevitably gets in the food?) or just the atmosphere, the preparation and eating experience is a cherished remembrance.

BAJA ADOBO is formulated to mimic that special flavor (but without the sand.) Though the beach may be many miles away, *BAJA ADOBO* adds a taste that can only be defined as that *"California Flavor."*

An exclusive and careful combination of salt, garlic, oregano, black pepper and 4 other spices, *BAJA ADOBO* brings that wonderful *"cooked right on the beach"* flavor to each dish you prepare. Your friends will think you have been taking cooking lessons.

BAJA ADOBO is delicious for seasoning all meat and seafood dishes and is a wonderful addition to gravies, vegetables, soups and salads.

DEEP SOUTH SOUL

On a driving trip to Florida many years ago I stopped at a small café on a side road in Mississippi for a mid-afternoon lunch. On the menu was a dish my grandmother cooked that I would not eat when I was a young boy; "collards."

When I tried them they were wonderful, and I asked the lady what in the world she put in them to make them taste so good, she smiled a beautiful smile as she replied, *"Son, I put soul in them greens."* I never forgot that statement.

With the success of the original spices, I resolved to recreate that delicious flavor. An inimitable combination of salt, ground red & green bell peppers, onion, garlic, paprika and 7 other spices, *SOUL* adds flavor to soups and stews; boosts the taste to cooked or raw vegetables and (of course) all greens; and adds zest to sandwiches.

After using just once, you will find that *SOUL* is an essential for mashed potatoes and salads and will bring smiles of delight to every member of your family as you put a little *"south in their mouth."*

SOUL is another favorite to use on cottage cheese.

CUBAN

Continuing to look for original seasonings, I decided to create a combination of ingredients that would mimic the flavors of Southeastern Cuba. In a two-year sojourn there over 50 years ago, I came to appreciate the distinctive flavors of Cuban cooking.

In Guantanamo City there was a small family restaurant where the proprietress would prepare huge steaks on a brazier in an open courtyard just outside the dining area. The aroma would permeate the whole place and add to the enjoyment of the meal. *CUBAN* will introduce you to the distinguishing flavor of food that, at least in those days could be found there.

After completing the first formulation of salt, sage, onion, garlic, Mexican oregano and 8 other spices, I tested it on a steak prepared on my grill. The smell and taste took me back to those years I spent in Cuba.

CUBAN is not only is it great for steaks on the grill, did pass my palate. When I asked the lady who served but also for roasts in the oven and all other meats. Used in moderation, it is great in stews and soups, vegetables and salads and just about any other recipe to which you want to add some pizzazz.

BBQ PAT

I had always wanted to barbeque brisket, ribs and other meats and fish but had not gotten around to doing it. Then in 2001 my cousin from Springfield, Missouri, gifted me with a smoker for Christmas. I let it sit around for three months before assembling it and trying it out.

My first attempt was a brutal learning lesson. The meat was tough and the flavor was dull. I did several things wrong. I had cooked at too high a temperature for too short a time, and the rub I used had too much salt in it. Changing the temperature and cooking time was easy to resolve, but the seasoning was another thing.

I tested each of the seasonings I had already formulated, but none gave me the flavor I was looking for; so I set out to formulate a new one. After four or five attempts, I finally hit on the right blend of salt, brown sugar, paprika, onion and chipotle; then enhanced them with 17 other spices.

There are many meat *rubs* on the market, each marketed toward a specific meat with the connotation that you have to '*rub*' the meat to get it to penetrate. *BBQ PAT* is so unique it amplifies the flavor of *every* meat *(including game and seafood)*. Just sprinkle liberally on meat and *'PAT'* so it adheres.

It is best when used in a smoker, but is great for grilling and even imparts a special flavor when cooking in your oven.

ARGENTINEAN

The early settlers of Argentina came mostly from countries bordering the Mediterranean sea, bringing the spices known to them. Combining them with the native herbes familiar to the Inca's brought into existance a whole new flavor. While about a third settled into cities along the coast, the others moved westward to the Pampas and the natural barrier of the Andes.

The Argentine flavor may be referred to as a cultural blending between these Mediterranean influences (such as the one exerted by Italian-Spanish and Arabic populations) and the Incan uses of indigenous herbs.

From the land of the gaucho *ARGENTINEAN* brings the smoky taste of the pampas to enhance the flavor of every dish you serve. Featuring a combination of salt, tomato powder, brown sugar, granulated onion, Mexican paprika, and 8 other spices. *ARGENTINEAN* is also great on beef, pork, chicken, veal and lamb.

NEW MEXICO CHIPOTLE

My introduction to the flavors of New Mexico came on a driving business trip in the early 1970's. From Tucumcari to Albuquerque I had driven in a snow storm and arrived early in the evening. Though the heater had worked perfectly, I still felt cold and thought a good bowl of chili would warm me.

When I placed my order, the waitress asked, "Red or green?" I didn't want to exhibit my lack of knowledge so answered "red." What

I got was a bowl of stewed 'green chilies' with about a double tablespoon of ground meat floating around among them.

This began my love affair with green chilies which grew into an appreciation of all the chilies grown and used in New Mexico.

From the "land of enchantment" comes a superb blend of the finest peppers and spices; and *NEW MEXICO CHIPOTLE* will enhance the flavor of every food you prepare.

Formulated using salt, chipotle, paprika, powdered green chilies, red & green bell peppers, garlic, and 12 other spices.

NEW ZEALAND SEAFOOD

The first to arrive in New Zealand were most likely the Polynesians, sometime in the 1300's. They would have brought with them limited quantities of food and such spices as were available on their home islands.

There being a limited animal population they subsisted mostly on the bounties of the sea. The Europeans began arriving in numbers during the late 1700's, and today, over 129 species of edible fish are commercially harvested.

In honor of the *'land down under'* comes a south pacific taste from an ideal blend of spices to enhance the flavor of fish, oysters, scallops and shrimp. My favorite is *NEW ZEALAND* seasoned orange Roughy cooked on the grill.

Carefully concocted measures of salt, granulated garlic, onion powder, sugar, citric acid, black pepper and 9 other spices, *NEW ZEALAND* is also great for all fresh-water fish and wonderful in gumbos, soups & dips.

TASTE OF TUSCANY

Oh Italia! How much I do enjoy visiting you. Our first trip was such a revelation. Arriving late in the day, picking up the rental car and driving into the city caused me to use all of the navigational and map reading skills I have acquired though my life. I found the street the hotel was located on and began looking for the street number. A challenge at any time, but particularly so when the street names were only on the corners of the buildings and sometimes missing altogether. And then, to compound the problem, the street names changed about every 3 to 5 blocks.

But oh the food!

Being central to the ancient trade routes, the Italians have taken full advantage of the abundance of spices available to them.

Having not found the proper combination of spices that fully reflect the wonderful tastes of Tuscany cooking, I undertook to compound an appropriate formula to please the palates of even native Italians.

You will have to decide for yourself if proportionally mixing salt, flake onion, red & green bell peppers, parsley, garlic and 7 other spices brings you the anticipated flavor of your own desires.

I dearly love this spice on my tomato soup.

CHILEAN SEAFOOD

From the waters along the coast of the most westerly country in South America comes a multitude of fishes that are delightful to the taste buds.

Chilean Sea Bass is probably the best known, and though also found around New Zealand, Australia and the Falklands, the demand is beginning to cause over-fishing.

Fortunately, fish farming this delicious fare is beginning to grow which could relieve some of the stress.

CHILEAN SEAFOOD will amplify the flavor of not only Chilean Sea Bass, but any seafood or fresh water fish you use it on. Though formulated to bring to perfection the flavors of fish, I erroneously grabbed it one evening and put it on the hamburgers I was grilling and found them to be delicious.

Compounded using salt, chipotle powder, paprika, sugar, ground red & green chilies, ground red bell pepper and 19 other spices.

Try it in soups, stews and gumbos. Even adds a distinctive flavor to salads.

HERBES DE LANGUEDOC

When friends invited us to visit them in their restored ruins in the village of Vieussan in southern France, I had no idea the trip would result in a new seasoning.

On a previous trip to France I had become acquainted with *Herbes de Provence* and came to love the flavors they imparted to many dishes.

The Languedoc area lies in the medieval part of France (10th to 13th centuries), and roughly covers the region between the Rhone and the Aude River, borders the Mediterranean and extends northwards to the Cévennes and the Massif Central. The herbs that grow here are natural to the area and grow in profusion. They were used by kings and serfs to enhance the flavor of their food. They continue to be used today by those with discriminating taste.

The growth and flavor of herbs in the Languedoc area is much like the growth and flavor of wines in the area. Everything contributes to the flavors; the soil, climate, amount of sun, rain and shade; the steepness of the hillside or flatness of the land. In France, these combinations of attributes are called the "terroir".

Herbs grow wild everywhere in the Languedoc area. The hillsides are covered with brush and herbs called the "garrigue". When you walk through the woods, you can smell the fragrance of the herbs all around you. And of course, when you step on them or brush against them, you release their magnificent fragrance.

HERBES DE LANGUEDOC is a blend of thyme, rosemary, marjoram, basil, lavender and 11 other spices, the flavor of each dish you use in on or in will be enhanced to its peak of perfection.

SICILLIAN SEAFOOD

Surrounded by the Mediterranean, it was only natural that seafood be a staple of the diet of the people who first settled there and is still important to the inhabitants of today.

When the Greeks saw the island of Sicily, they fell in love, sent their fleets, and set up colonies. The Romans saw what the Greeks had, fought them for it, and became the new conquerors.

From the every point of the compass came conquerors that saw the varied climates, abundance of fruits and vegetables and took the land for their own. With the armies came their seasonings and all are assimilated in Sicilian fare.

Mount Etna, a highly active volcano that destroys whatever is in the path of its lava eruptions also fertilizes the soil to incomparable richness. The crops that grow in this soil have no parallel. The quality of the vegetables gives a clue to the dishes of Sicily. Since their vegetables are of superior taste and quality, no Sicilian would defile them by over-seasoning.

We, on the other hand are not privileged to such foods and must rely on produce cultivated on a mass basis.

SICILIAN SEAFOOD provides its flavor from the careful mixing of salt, granulated onion, black pepper, red & green peppers, sugar and 15 other spices.

TABLE OF CONTENTS

RECIPES

APPETIZERS & DIPS

SAUCES & RELISHES

SEAFOOD

SIDE DISHES

SOUPS

SWEETS

POETRY

STORIES

PUPPIES, PONIES & PUSSY CATS

ABOUT THE AUTHOR

Lee Douglas brings a wealth of experience to his writing and speaking career. From Pilot to Preacher to Poet; Sales Executive to Computer System Designer; School Teacher to Sales Trainer; Construction to Consultant; Inventor to Innovator, his varied background has provided him exposure to people from many walks and ways of life.

He has written and produced 15 training videos for Panasonic and Tandy Corporation, produced a Television show for a local Dallas TV station, and written, directed and produced a feature family film.

As Super-Seller of Products, Ideas and Dreams, Lee is the consummate storyteller and is at his best when bringing stories to life in rhyme, formulating spices or creating new recipes.

In a career in life insurance sales, Lee acquired the art of leading people to see beyond their current circumstances to bring their future into focus.

In his career in computer system design, he learned to give attention to the minutest detail to insure the proper fitting together of each element.

As director of operations of the Data Processing department for a large national company, he developed his organizational skills.

In his dealing with people he has a talent for leading them to recognize and perform up to their potential.

He got into cooking when he invented a line of baking products, Dr. Douglas' Wonder Bakers®, and was told by the distributor he needed to develop recipes to accompany them.

Soon he began experimenting by combining various spices in unique ways and his line of spices is one of the results. He has a refined sense of taste that leads to combinations of spices that are reminiscent of the areas after which he has named them.

Down Home Seasonings which are available at:

www.downhomespices.com